The Making of Tools

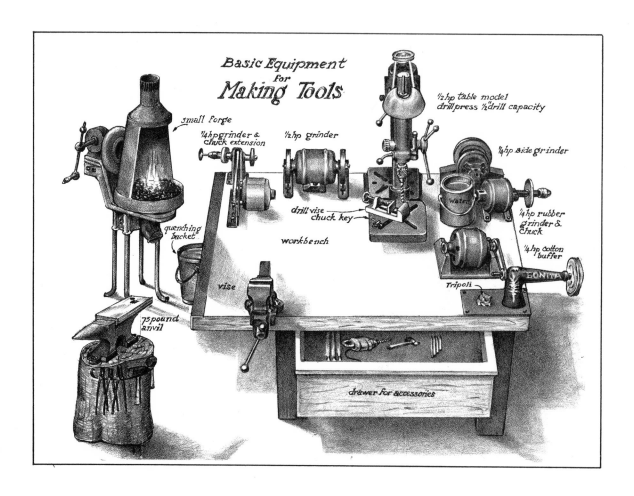

Basic Equipment
for
Making Tools

small forge

¼ hp grinder &
chuck extension

½ hp grinder

½ hp table model
drill press ½" drill capacity

¼ hp side grinder

drill vise
chuck key

quenching
bucket

water

workbench

¼ hp rubber
grinder &
chuck

¼ hp cotton
buffer

vise

Tripoli

BONITA

75 pound
anvil

drawer for accessories

The Making of Tools

ALEXANDER G. WEYGERS

Illustrations by the Author

VNR VAN NOSTRAND REINHOLD COMPANY
New York   Cincinnati   Toronto   London   Melbourne

Van Nostrand Reinhold Company Regional Offices:
New York   Cincinnati   Chicago   Millbrae   Dallas

Van Nostrand Reinhold Company International Offices:
London   Toronto   Melbourne

Copyright © 1973 by Litton Educational Publishing, Inc.

Library of Congress Catalog Card Number 72-7847

ISBN 0 442-29360-7 (paper)
ISBN 0 442-29361-5 (cloth)

Designed by Morris Karol

Published by Van Nostrand Reinhold Company
450 West 33rd Street, New York, N. Y. 10001

16 15 14 13 12 11 10 9 8 7 6 5 4

Contents

INTRODUCTION 7

1. A Beginner's Workshop 8

Installation of Equipment 8
THE WORKBENCH 8 / THE BENCH
VISE 9 / THE DRILL PRESS 9 /
ACCESSORIES TO THE DRILL PRESS 10 /
THE ½ HP GRINDER 10 / TOOL RESTS
11 / THE ¼ HP GRINDER AND CHUCK
EXTENSION 11 / THE ¼ HP BUFFER
11 / THE COTTON BUFFER 12 /
BUFFING COMPOUND 12 / THE ¼
HP SIDE GRINDER AND SANDING DISCS
12 / THE ABRASIVE CUTOFF WHEEL
13 / THE RUBBER ABRASIVE WHEEL
13 / THE ANVIL 13 / THE
FORGE 13
Materials 14
HIGH-CARBON STEEL 14 / MILD
STEEL 14
The Quenching Bath 15
WATER 15 / BRINE 15 / OIL OR
LAMB'S FAT 15
Wood for Handles 16

2. Tempering Steel 17

Tests for Temperability 17
Tempering a Tool Blade 18
Coolant Temperature 18
Drawing Temper Colors 19
Case Hardening Steel 21
The Oxidation Color Spectrum 21
The Color Range of Hot Steel 22
HEAT-GLOW COLORS 22 /

3. Making the First Tool: A Screw Driver 23

4. Making a Cold Chisel and Other Simple Tools 25

A Cold Chisel 25
Shaping and Tempering the Cold
Chisel 25
A Center Punch 27
A Nail Set 27
Chasing Tools 27
Punches 27
A Paint Mixer 27
Drill Bits 27

5. Making Stonecarving Tools 28

The One-Point Tool 28
The Claw Tool 29
The Bush Tool 31

6. Sharpening Tools 32

Making a Side Grinder 32
Use of the Side Grinder 33
SALVAGING WORN STONES 33 / THE
DRESSING TOOL 33 / DRESSING WORN
GRINDING WHEELS 34 / DRESSING A
BROKEN GOUGE EDGE 34
The Rubber Abrasive Wheel 35
The Buffing Wheel 36
Use of Hand Stones 37
Sharpening a Carpenter's Chisel 38
GRINDING MOTIONS 38 / HONING THE
BURR 39 / STROPPING THE BURR 39
Sharpening Round Gouges 40
Use of the Dry Grinder 41
Testing for Sharpness 42

7. Making Carpenter's Chisels 43

The Narrow Chisel 43
The Broad-blade Chisel 43
Files as Stock for Chisels and
Lathe-Turning Tools 44

8. Making Cutting Tools 45

Knife for Cardboard and Paper 45
A Cherry Pitter 46

Garden Tools 47
Kitchen Cleaver 48

9. **Making Eyebolts and Hooks 49**

10. **Making Tool Handles 50**

Converting the Drill Press into
a Lathe 50
Stock for Tool Handles 51
Shaping the Handle 51
Ferrules 52
Fitting Handles to Ferrules 53
Finishing the Handle 53
Assembling Handle and Tool 54
Tempering the Tool Blade 54

11. **Making Hammers 55**

Hammer Design 55
HAMMER WEIGHT 55 / THE FACE
56 / THE CLAW 56 /
THE STEM 56
The Cross Peen Hammer 57

12. **Making Sculptor's Woodcarving
Gouges 60**

Design of the Sculptor's
Woodcarving Gouge 60
Small Woodcarving Gouges 61
A ⅛-INCH-DEEP GOUGE 62 / A WIDE-
BLADED ENGRAVER'S STYLE GOUGE 63 /
FINISHING GOUGES 63 / A V-SHAPED
GOUGE MADE BY FOLDING 64 /
SMALL-TOOL HANDLES 64 / A SMALL
V-SHAPED GOUGE 65
Large Woodcarving Gouges 66
GRINDING THE BEVEL 68 / REMOVING
THE BURR 69 / TEMPERING AND
ASSEMBLY 69

13. **Making a Seating Cutter and
Hinge Joints 70**

The Seating Cutter 70
Hinge Joints 71
MAKING A STRONG AND ACCURATE HINGE
JOINT 72 / ASSEMBLING THE HINGE
JOINT 72

14. **Making Tinsnips 74**

Light-Gauge Tinsnips 74
HOLLOW-GRINDING THE CUTTING
BLADES 75 / CURVING THE BLADES
76 / TEMPERING THE BLADES 76 /
DRAWING TEMPER COLORS 76
Heavy-Duty Tinsnips 77
THE HINGE 77

15. **Making Wire and Nail Cutters 78**

Narrow-jawed Cutters 78
Wide-jawed Cutters 79

16. **Making Large Shears 80**

17. **Making Pliers 82**

Plier Blanks 82
Tempering the Jaws 83
Aligning Jaws and Handles 84

18. **Applying Color Patina to
Steel Surfaces 85**

PHOTOGRAPHS 86 / HINTS ON
USING POWER TOOLS AND OTHER
ADMONITIONS 88
GLOSSARY 90

Introduction

This book teaches the artist and craftsman how to make his own tools: how to design, sharpen, and temper them.

Having made tools (for myself and for others) for most of my life, I have also enjoyed teaching this very rewarding craft, finding that anyone who is naturally handy can readily succeed in toolmaking. The student can begin with a minimum of equipment, at little expense. Using scrap steel (often available at no cost), he can start by making the simplest tools and gradually progress to more and more difficult ones. Once a student has learned to make his own tools, he will be forever independent of having to buy those not specifically designed for his purpose.

Many students, after three weeks of intensive training under my guidance, have produced sets of wood- and stonecarving tools as fine as my own. And, over the years, the students invariably observe that the value of the fine tools they have made during the short course exceeds the cost of their tuition. One might say they were taught for free, emerging as full-fledged toolmakers, each one carrying home a beautiful set of tools to boot.

The guidelines to toolmaking in this book are identical to the information and explanations I give in class. The drawings are "picture translations" of my personal demonstrations to students, showing the step-by-step progression from the raw material to the finished product — the handmade tool.

1. A Beginner's Workshop

A beginner's workshop ought to include the following basic equipment:

A sturdy workbench, onto which are bolted:

Grinder (¼ hp) and *chuck extension*

Dry grinding wheel assembly, based on a ½ hp motor grinder

Table-model drill press (½ hp; ½-inch-diameter drill capacity)

Side grinder (¼ hp)

Rubber abrasive wheel (¼ hp; can of water adjacent, to cool workpieces)

Buffer (¼ hp)

Vise (35-pound, or heavier)

Anvil (25-pound, or heavier; preferably mounted separately, on a freestanding wood stump)

A large drawer under bench, in which to store a cumulative collection of accessory tools: wrenches, files, drills, hammers, center punch, cold chisels, hacksaw, assorted grinding wheels, sanding discs, drill vise, and chuck key, etc.

A small forge, in which to shape and temper your tools (a forge is preferred, though a *charcoal brazier* will do). To draw temper color, use either a gas flame (as in a kitchen stove), a Bunsen burner, or the blue flame of a plumber's blowtorch fueled with gasoline.

A quenching bucket

A coal bin

This minimum workshop can be equipped very satisfactorily with secondhand articles, provided they are in good working order. Therefore, look for discarded washing-machine motors, surplus-store grinding wheels, hammers, files, etc. Flea markets and garage sales frequently will provide surprisingly useful items with which to complete your shop.

INSTALLATION OF EQUIPMENT

The Workbench

In nine out of ten hobby shops, workbenches are too flimsy. Instead, they should be as sturdy as possible, to support equipment which is put under great strain. Everything fastened to a *heavy* workbench benefits from its supporting mass and rigidity. Obviously, for instance, much energy will be wasted if hammer blows are delivered onto workpieces held in an insecure vise on a wobbly or lightweight bench.

The equipment arrangement here is mainly to guide those who have limited space in their workshop. A long, roomy bench built against a strong wall is the ideal arrangement: it allows the various machine units to be spaced out in the most workable and orderly way, while

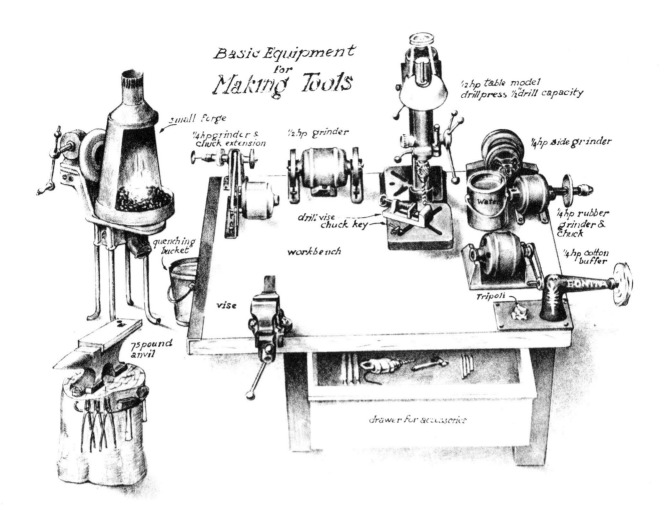

Basic Equipment for Making Tools

½hp table model drillpress ½"drill capacity

small forge

¼hp grinder & chuck extension

½hp grinder

¼hp side grinder

drill vise chuck key

water

¼hp rubber grinder & chuck

workbench

¼hp cotton buffer

quenching bucket

BONITA

vise

Tripoli

75 pound anvil

drawer for accessories

utilizing the wall as additional reinforcement. (Make sure though, that noise will not carry through the wall and disturb neighbors.)

The Bench Vise

The vise shown is not adjustable at its base, but those that are — ones that can be turned around and clamped at any angle — ought to be bolted at the exact corner of the bench.

Bench vises should not weigh less than twenty-five pounds — and the heavier, the better; with luck, you may even find a good secondhand seventy-five-pound monster. Large vises, with wider jaws, can hold bigger workpieces, a great advantage when woodcarvings are to be clamped in them.

The Drill Press

As the most important piece of equipment in your shop, the drill press should not be smaller than that shown here. Bolted onto the bench, its swivel table should be adjustable in every position, and high enough in its lowest position to clear all permanent bench machinery when a long workpiece is clamped on it.

A versatile machine, the drill press can do routing, filing, rasping, and grinding, in addition to the drilling it is designed to do. It can also be adapted to function as a wood lathe (see Chapter 10). Once you become familiar with the drill press, your own inventiveness will find many uses for it.

Accessories to the Drill Press

In addition to assorted metal- and wood-cutting drills stored in the bench drawer, one major accessory is the drill-press vise (as shown). Placed on the drill press's swivel base, it is used to hold a workpiece that has previously been marked by a center punch. Firmly held in the vise, it prevents the drill from wandering off these marks.

A speed-reduction attachment for your drill press is very useful, if you can afford one. For much heavy-duty work, large drills should be slowed down, to save wear and tear on both drills and press.

Other small tools, such as routers, rotary files and rasps, drum sanders and grinding points, special woodcutters, chuck inserts for special tasks, and various others will gradually be added to your basic drill-press equipment.

As you will be learning to make many of these accessory tools yourself as you proceed, try to resist the temptation to buy them before they are needed.

The ½ hp Grinder

This grinder is the next most important piece of equipment for your workbench.

If you use a fast 3600 rpm electric motor, it is safest to have the grinding wheels not larger than 6 inches in diameter. A slower motor of 1750 rpm may safely have wheels up to 8 inches in diameter and not less than ¾ inch thick. These safety factors are purposely more severe than those required by industry because we shall eliminate the wheelguards in order to have maximum access to the fully exposed wheels.

It should be noted that *extreme caution* is needed when using a high-speed electric motor. While you may be tempted to use one should it come your way, you should realize that it is much safer to work with slower-speed tools in hobby shops. Injury can occur if instruments are inserted off-center when cutting, grinding, or rubbing. Centrifugal force — greater at high speed than at low — may cause inaccurate instruments to fly apart, bend, and whip around, causing serious bodily harm. A little less speed equals a little more safety, and you can still progress fast enough, since the machine saves time and muscle.

All rough work (requiring a large quantity of metal removal by means of grinding) should be done on the ½ hp unit, using coarse, hard, and thick stones. If you decide to buy a new motor, choose a model with a double-shaft arbor like the one shown, which is designed to receive a grinding wheel on each end of the shaft.

First, place an extension adapter on the shaft as shown. Secure it firmly with two setscrews, which should be tightly seated in $1/16$-inch-deep holes and tightened with an Allen-wrench key. These adapters, in turn, are to hold a 6-inch wheel, 2 inches thick, fixed

¼ hp electric motors sufficient for toolmaking tasks

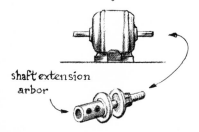

shaft extension arbor

between washers and nuts. (I have threaded my motor shafts to eliminate the need for adapters, using washers and nuts to lock wheels. As both ends of the shaft have right-hand threads, the left-hand wheel must be locked with two nuts, since, when it rotates toward you during grinding, it tends to loosen itself.

Tool Rests

Bolted separately on the bench below the wheels, tool rests are adjustable simply by tapping the hammer against them to close the gap that forms as the wheels are worn down (especially after redressing the wheels). If it seems too difficult to make this tool rest, have a welding shop do it for you.

The ¼ hp Grinder and Chuck Extension

This grinding unit is used mainly to receive chuck inserts of small caliber, which do the more refined grinding, sanding, and polishing, especially of delicate tools.

Since ¼ hp electric motors of 1750 rpm are standard in household utility machines such as laundry- and dishwashers, these motors are often discarded or available secondhand. As some have odd foundation bolts through silencing rubber cushions, a little inventiveness is called for in mounting them. With the one shown here, I simply tap a hammer against the frame on which the motor is bolted; this tightens the belt whenever necessary, even with the motor running.

The ¼ hp Buffer

Here, the ¼ hp motor (one salvaged, without bolt holes or base) is cradled in two wooden blocks and strapped down with a piece of band steel. The blocks, in turn, are screwed on a plywood baseboard, and the entire assembly is then hinged onto the bench. This method allows the motor's weight to "hang" in the belt, thus automatically keeping the belt tightened against slippage.

Sometimes, a slight unevenness in the belt (or a slightly eccentric pulley) can cause vibration. The motor baseboard can then be anchored to the workbench with a long wood screw, which steadies it but still allows some play.

adjust toolrest

chuck

sanding

chuck inserts

grinding

filing

rasping

weight of motor tightens belt

polishing (buffing)

buffing compound

the side grinder

sanding disc

The Cotton Buffer

The 8- to 10-inch-diameter cotton buffing wheel is mounted on the shaft of a housing salvaged from an old-fashioned sewing machine. Stripped of its other parts with hacksaw or abrasive cutoff wheel, this housing is screwed onto a steel base plate, which, in turn, is bolted to one corner of the workbench. This positioning allows maximum access to the buffing wheel.

If this type of shop-made buffing unit seems too much of an undertaking at the outset, compromise by purchasing a ready-made buffer on a small shaft as a chuck insert; then clamp it in the drill press chuck or in the chuck on the extension of one of the ¼ hp grinding units. Such chuck inserts are readily available in hardware stores, mail-order houses, or through hobbyists' catalogs.

Buffing Compound

The best buffing compound is an abrasive wax mix called *tripoli*, found in any hardware store. Choose coarse grit for toolmaking jobs. A one- or two-pound block of tripoli, held against the rapidly rotating cotton buffer, momentarily melts the wax in the mix and thus adheres to the buffer. Once cooled and hardened, the coated buffer becomes a polishing tool, as well as a mechanical sharpening strop. It will buff all finely ground steel mirror-smooth, and, in short, prove altogether indispensable in your toolmaking.

The ¼ hp Side Grinder and Sanding Discs

This grinder is built from a discarded motor and an industrial cutoff-wheel remnant.

Steel-construction plants use cutoff wheels that are made from an abrasive mix, sometimes fiber-bonded to make them shatterproof. When new, they measure approximately 24 inches in diameter and ⅛ inch to $^3/_{16}$ inch thick. They are clamped between 6- to 8-inch-diameter washers. When they become worn down to about 10 inches in diameter, so little remains outside the washer to cut with that a new wheel must replace it and the remnant becomes a waste product.

If you can locate a steel-construction plant nearby that uses this cutting method, they will surely have some 8- to 10-inch discards to give you or sell for little. (See Chapter 6 for making a side grinder.)

If you have a table saw, you can mount side-grinding abrasive discs on it in place of the saw blade. First, remove all sawdust that might be ignited by sparks coming from the disc. Second, be sure to protect your machine from abrasive dust that might reach any bearings that have not been properly sealed. Such discs are, as a rule, made of $^3/_{16}$-inch-thick steel, to which is glued a tough sheet of coarse- or fine-grit abrasive.

Another side grinder setup employs a slightly flexible, plastic-bonded abrasive disc as a chuck-insert accessory. Several kinds are offered in hardware stores; their advantage is that the whole disc can be utilized, instead of only the half rotating above the saw table.

The Abrasive Cutoff Wheel

If you have an 8- to 10-inch circular table saw, mounting an abrasive cutoff wheel in place of the saw blade will enable you to cut hardened steel. This piece of equipment becomes a great help early in your toolmaking education, especially if scrap steel is to be your major source of material. All hardened steel can be cut cleanly with it, without having to anneal the steel beforehand.

abrasive cut off wheel

The Rubber Abrasive Wheel

The rubber abrasive wheel is indispensable but difficult to master. A coarse-grit, 6- to 7-inch-diameter wheel, ½- to ¾-inch-thick, is good enough; a 1750 rpm salvaged washing-machine motor is fast enough. Mount it between washers on a ½-inch-diameter standard extension shaft, thus leaving room, after mounting the rubber wheel, for a standard ½-inch auxiliary chuck, if needed. Both extension shaft and chuck are available at hardware stores that handle power tools and their accessories.

rubber abrasive wheel

The potential harm that can come to the rubber abrasive wheel as well as to yourself must never be ignored or underestimated (this is described at length in Chapter 6). It can be perfectly safely used once its correct handling is clearly understood, and its advantages outweigh both the risk of accident and any consequent cost of repair. Its careful use, once mastered, can produce wondrous results.

The Anvil

A small anvil is shown here. Anvils must be bolted onto a freestanding wood stump next to your forge. Ideally, anvil, forge, and water-quenching trough should be clustered in the darkest corner of your shop (for only in the semi-dark should you attempt to judge the color of heated steel).

correct height of anvil face from floor level

The Forge

An old, or even antique, little outdoor riveting forge is excellent for a beginner's shop. Blacksmith coal, which can be bought wherever horseshoers still ply their trade, is the ideal fuel. Feed-and-fuel stores in farming communities usually carry blacksmith coal. Although coke is a good fuel, too, I have never found a source for it.

Professional metal-working shops often have gas-fired forges, but for a beginning toolmaker, such a forge has several drawbacks. It is very noisy, since a forced-air blast is used to reach high heat; the large opening of the fire grate (about 1 by 3 inches) lets small forgings drop through accidentally; and steel oxidizes at a prodigious rate in such fires. In contrast, the regular coal-fired forge has a cast-iron grating (needing only six to ten ⅜-inch air holes), and creates very little steel oxidization. Also, the "carbon" character of coal tends to improve the steel rather than deteriorate it.

Other acceptable means of heating steel include acetylene torches, outdoor barbecue braziers, wood stoves, and fireplaces.

MATERIALS

High-Carbon Steel

Most tools are made of high-carbon steel. This is *temperable* steel. It can be bought cheaply at steel scrapyards and automobile junkyards. And, once you develop an eye for it, great amounts are found strewn along highways and in vacant lots to add to your own scrap pile. No matter how beat-up or rusty a piece of discarded scrap may be, add it to your supply. Scrap is cheap, and as rusty, corroded surfaces are usually only skin-deep, they can easily be ground clean.

Your first trip for material should be to nearby dealers in scrap steel. If they permit you to roam over their yard, search particularly for all kinds of *spring steel:* leaf springs and coil springs of cars, garage-door springs, springs from garden swings, some heavy-gauge truck engine valve springs, broken starter springs, torsion bars, and stick-shift arms — any discarded machine parts that you suspect may be made of high-carbon steel — all contribute to your toolmaking supply. (Chapter 2 explains how to "test" steel for high-carbon quality.)

Note that spring steel has a sufficiently high carbon content that it can be tempered for hard cutting edges such as cold chisels. But the temper hardness used in car springs, though not hard enough for a cold chisel, often is hard enough for wood lathe-turning tools and wood chisels (if the wood to be worked is not too hard).

While many high-carbon steels have varying degrees of metals mixed through them, such as molybdenum, vanadium, tungsten, or other alloy additives, all such high-carbon steels are temperable, which is your main concern.

The question now is: Are all those different steels to be tempered differently? The more experience you gain in toolmaking, the more you come to realize that an "average" tempering method is practical for most of these steels, regardless of any scientifically prescribed tempering charts which list exact procedures for heat-treating (tempering) various alloy steels in industry.

If you decide at the outset to "make do" with the endless, unknown high-carbon steel varieties on scrap piles, it is the empirical (trial-and-error) methods set forth in this book that are to be followed. If you decide to make fine tools from scrap steel of unknown quality, then it is this type of steel that you must speculate about and deal with.

I can assure you that during the fifty years that I have made tools from questionable types of high-carbon steels, a very large percentage of these tools turned out to be excellent, and all of them have stood up under hard use — and often abuse as well. So don't worry if you feel that you know nothing about steel; you will learn enough as you work and practice.

Mild Steel

Such steel is of a low-carbon content and is not temperable, although its surface layer can be hardened through a process called *case hardening,* which applies a skin-deep hardness (see Chapter 2). Some tools can be made of mild steel, such as those that do not require hard-cutting or long-wearing parts (some garden tools, for instance).

From the same sources that produced high-carbon steel scrap can be found mild-steel plates, rods, and bars. All can be made into useful articles. In short, any and all steel parts you believe might be valuable in your metalworking activities are welcome, and tests in the shop will distinguish one steel from the other.

THE QUENCHING BATH

This bath may consist of water, brine, oil, or fat. Plain water for steel-tempering has been my choice all these years, but others find a salt brine, or other blacksmith-recommended quenching liquids, more desirable. I simply offer my own experience, recognizing, however, that the other liquids work as well. The merits of each different one are explained further when we discuss tempering (see Chapter 2).

Water

Water should be kept next to the forge. A water bucket will do, but a rectangular metal container is better. It should not be smaller than 10 by 24 inches and 15 to 20 inches deep, in order to quench long workpieces.

A tin can nailed to the end of a branch or stick makes a douser, and twenty-five or more little holes punched through its bottom with a small, sharp nail turns the dipper into a water sprinkler. This sprinkler keeps the coal surrounding the fire wet, and holds it to just the size of fire needed. Also, it is used occasionally to cool the steel workpiece that extends *outside* the fire by dousing it while the rest remains in the fire undisturbed. It is especially useful, then, to douse handheld steel rods that are rather short and thus may heat up through conductivity.

Because water is always nearby, fires are seldom started by accident in a blacksmith shop. The smith is always there when the forge is fired up, and can dip into the water trough in case a piece of hot steel or coal should be dropped on sawdust, wood, or fabric.

Brine

Brine is made by saturating water with common rock salt. The right amount of salt is determined by experimentation. The more salt-saturated the water, the higher the temperature at its boiling point. Some people have quenched a hot tool tip in powdered salt, with good results; such pure salt melts at a temperature much higher than the boiling point of brine or oil.

Oil or Lamb's Fat

Have some old motor oil on hand in a five-gallon can (covered, to avoid flash fires), for general use.

Rendered lamb's fat should be used to harden all very small, delicate tools. If possible, have as much as one gallon handy, kept in a lidded can to keep rodents away. This type of fat leaves the steel surface remarkably clean, while old motor oil often deposits some black carbon scale on the quenched steel; though it requires extra work to remove it, such deposits are otherwise harmless.

Historically, blacksmiths have always had this choice of quenching liquids: I believe it has caused many varied recommendations on how to temper steel, with as many varied results.

In due time, each smith naturally becomes convinced that, at long last, he has found the "best" way. Still, he often suspects that another smith may just have a secret recipe in *his* technique that he is not sharing. What could it be? It opens the door to mystery for the romantic craftsman. And there *is* romance in forming hot and malleable steel, then changing it into very hard steel. As makers of tools, we are bound to enter into endless exploration: using all sorts of steel; forming it into many shapes; tempering it in a variety of ways.

WOOD FOR HANDLES

A straight-grained, hard (not too brittle), tough wood is best for tool handles. Black and English walnut, hickory, ash, eucalyptus — all respond favorably. And don't hesitate to test wood that grows locally which you suspect might be suitable.

Many other materials will be needed in your toolmaking, such as grinding compounds, abrasive papers and grinding stones, steel tubing for ferrules, etc. They can all be added from time to time as they are needed.

2. Tempering Steel

Only *high-carbon* steels are temperable and can be hardened in the process called tempering. Mild, or low-carbon, steel cannot be tempered but may be case-hardened. Hardened tool edges must cut, shear, punch, emboss, and do many other tasks demanding both hardness and toughness. Such tools must not break or bend in normal use. The aim should be that tool edges, in well-designed and well-tempered tools, should stand up, even under momentary extra strain.

The methods for tempering recommended in this book are based on what I believe are the most reliable and practical when you work with scrap steel. Scrap piles are bound to contain a great variety of high-carbon steels from different machine and car parts. Such varieties, as a rule, react well to my tempering methods because of their high-carbon content, *not* because other metals have been added to produce special alloy steels.

Manufacturers' precise tempering procedures vary somewhat from mine because of the specialized industrial uses of alloy steels. Yet, in learning by trial and error, occasionally some high-carbon steels respond less favorably to my recommended methods.

An example of this would occur when making a cutting tool out of steel originally designed to remain fairly hard even under red-hot heat (such as automobile exhaust valves). Generally, the hardness of exhaust-valve steel remains *below* the hardness required for the cutting edges of our tools. Therefore, for any piece of steel, a test for temperability is always advised before you begin making a tool that must have a hardened and tough cutting edge.

TESTS FOR TEMPERABILITY

Test 1. From the scrap pile choose a steel rod that you suspect may be of a high-carbon quality. Hold it on the power grinder and examine the sparks; compare them with the sparks shown in the illustration, which distinguishes high- from low-carbon steel by spark characteristics. The rule of thumb in the shop is that a dull spark is mild steel, and a brilliant, sharply exploding spark is high-carbon steel. Most libraries have books you can examine showing the spark characteristics of various steels. If you still are not certain that the steel sample is of high-carbon quality, you can resort to the following sure and final test.

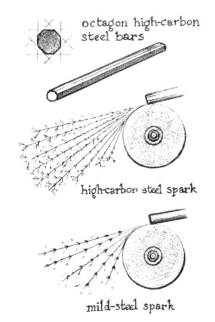

octagon high-carbon steel bars

high-carbon steel spark

mild-steel spark

heat to light cherry

quench

test for hardness with
file tip

heat range for tempering

heat to light cherry-red

Test 2. Build a medium-hot "clean" fire. (A "dirty" fire is any fire which emits smoke and yellow flame. It is an indication that combustible gases remain which may damage hot steel.) It should resemble a glowing charcoal fire.

Place the first inch of the rod horizontally in this fire, making sure that hot coals are always underneath the steel, as well as around and above it, to prevent fresh air from hitting it directly and thus oxidizing its surface. As soon as it heats up to a light cherry red glow (as judged in a semi-dark room), pull the rod out and immediately quench it completely in water at room temperature. It should emerge pearl gray in color.

Next, clamp the steel rod in the vise and, using the tip of a sharp file, pick on the gray quenched end. If the file tip slides off, like a needle on glass, it means that this steel is of high-carbon quality and thus temperable.

Various hardnesses of steel will be described separately and become more meaningful as we proceed in the practice of tool-tempering.

TEMPERING A TOOL BLADE

Once a tool blank made from tested steel is finished (as is the wood-carving gouge illustrated here), the blade can be tempered.

As described earlier, place the blade in a clean fire, gently fanning it to maintain an even, medium heat. Keep your eye on the tool, which is partly visible through the fire, but do not disturb the coals or the tool until you see that the blade has become light cherry red in color (again, as judged in a semi-dark room). My experience has been that, once the tool becomes invisible in the identical cherry-red glow of the fire, it is ready to be quenched.

When you are satisfied with the tool's color, withdraw it and immediately quench, holding it fully submerged and motionless in one of the following coolants:

Water, if the blade is fairly *thick*

Brine, if the blade is fairly *thin*

Oil (or rendered fat), if the blade is *very* thin

Rendered lamb's fat is ideally suited for tempering small, light-gauge tools.

COOLANT TEMPERATURE

All coolants should be kept at room temperature, to ensure that sufficient shock impact takes place here between the light cherry red heat glow of the blade and the room temperature of the quenching liquid. This shock impact produces the same outer hardness in the steel, no matter which coolant we choose.

While the boiling point of the liquid mantle that envelops the hot steel differs with each individual coolant, all coolants remain approximately at room temperature outside the hot mantle. Remember, therefore, that:

If the coolant is *water,* this mantle boils at approximately 100°C (212°F), cooling the steel toward the core *fastest.*

If the coolant is *brine,* this mantle boils at approximately 107°C (226°F) or thereabouts, depending on the concentration of salt in the brine, cooling the steel toward the core a little *slower.*

If the coolant is *oil or fat,* this mantle boils at approximately 150°C (290° F), cooling the steel toward the core *slowest.*

The importance of the choice of quenching liquid becomes clear

18

once you know that the slower the hot steel cools, the "softer" its core becomes. This inside "softness" creates the tool toughness needed to keep the tool from breaking. At the same time, it should be noted that outer hardness penetrates deeper in fastest-cooling water than in slowest-cooling oil. Steel cools, through conductivity, at a pace dictated by the boiling temperature of the liquid mantle as well as by the steel's coefficient of conductivity. The result is that:

In *water,* the core becomes only a little less hard (fast cooling).
In *brine,* the core is a little softer (slower cooling).
In *oil,* the core is softer still (slowest cooling).

You can now see that the kind of tool you are making will dictate your choice of quenching liquid. For very thin and delicate tools, therefore, an oil quench is advised. Its slowest cooling toward the core makes the tool as tough as possible, reducing the chance of the steel cracking because of too-fast cooling and shrinkage. Moreover, in thin, delicate tool blades, the outer hardness penetrates deep enough during slower cooling to make the steel uniformly hard all the way through.

Such steel emerges with the clean pearl-gray color of a new file, and with a file's brittle hardness, as shown here.

Put a sheen on the surface of the brittle area with the fine-grit abrasives in your shop. A final polish on the cotton buffer, using tripoli compound, will make the blade shine like a mirror. This is desirable because it allows you to see the slightest change in *oxidation colors* during the heating.

DRAWING TEMPER COLORS

To "draw" color is the term used for the process of reheating a brittle, hard steel in order to temper it for a specific hardness. As steel heats, its shiny surface changes color, and each color change indicates a change in steel hardness. Specific color thus "matches" specific hardness.

Use a standard commercial propane torch or a plumber's gasoline blowtorch. The blue flame of a kitchen gas range functions well, provided you fit a bent coffee can over the burner to concentrate the flame, as with a Bunsen burner. Another method is to place two firebricks, spaced ½ to 1 inch apart, on top of the forge fire, so that heat escaping between the bricks becomes a localized heat column.

Now begin to heat the tool shank, holding it in the blue flame. Keep the mirror-smooth, brittle *blade* safely *outside* the flame. Soon, as the gradually increasing heat of the shank is conducted toward the blade, the first oxidation color appears — a *faint straw yellow* (see color chart).

As you heat the steel further, you will see the whole color spectrum appear as a full color band: *blue,* nearest the flame, followed by the full oxidation color spectrum as shown, to, finally, the original sheen. When this full color band moves down the shank to the beginning of the blade part, now hold that part quite high above the visible flame, trying to visualize the invisible heat column rising from it.

It is in this less-hot region that you should now hold the blade — quite high at first, playing it safe. Within about a minute, in that position, an even change of oxidation (temper) color is drawn over the total area of the shiny blade. It will be a faint straw color.

If this change of color appears at the extreme outer edge first, it means heat is entering that thin area too fast. Either move the blade slightly off-center in the visualized heat column, or hold the tool higher

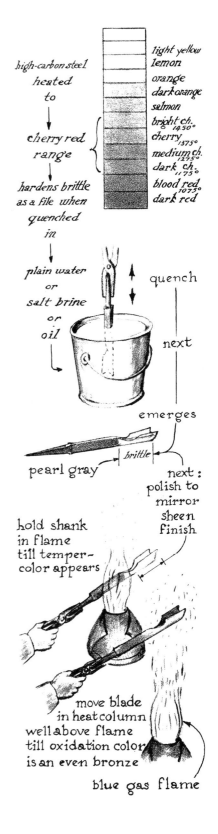

high-carbon steel
heated
to
↓
cherry red
range
↓
hardens brittle
as a file when
quenched
in
↓
plain water
or
salt brine
or
oil
↓

light yellow
lemon
orange
dark orange
salmon
bright ch. 1450°
cherry 1375°
medium ch. 1275°
dark ch. 1175°
blood red 1075°
dark red

quench
next
emerges

pearl gray   brittle   next:
polish to
mirror
sheen
finish

hold shank
in flame
till temper-
color appears

move blade
in heat column
well above flame
till oxidation color
is an even bronze

blue gas flame

still, to reduce heat as well as speed of heat transfer. Continue thus to manipulate the tool, holding it now here, now there. This controls the speed of heat transfer, the exact area to be tempered, and the precise moment for quenching at correct temper color.

The following guidelines will help you select correct temper colors during the hardening of various tools:

Peacock. For thin delicate tools, and tools with spring-action parts that are hand-pushed.

Bronze. For heavier-gauge woodcarving gouges that are struck with hammers.

Dark straw. For center punches, small cold chisels, etc.

Light straw. For blunt-edged sturdy tools, such as large cold chisels, star drills, bush tools, etc.

Unexpected things, over which you may have little control, will probably happen. For example, after a water quench, some steels emerge brittle-hard with such great tension that, if not tempered within a short time, they may crack lengthwise all by themselves. Such steels probably were designed to be hardened in oil, and manufacturers' manuals *do* refer to water-hardening and oil-hardening steels. Therefore, the unknown (and unknowable) elements in your scrap pile can leave you guessing somewhat.

To summarize and underscore the tempering steps, reexamine the oxidation color spectrum and the annealing of a steel bar as shown in the drawings, as well as the color chart. (See also the cover illustrations.)

From my experience in dealing with high-carbon scrap steel, much that is hardened in oil shrinks less than that quenched in water or brine. And, as the tension that weakens steel is still further reduced during tempering in oil, it is wisest for delicate, thin tools to be hardened in oil or lamb's fat.

The many variables involved here in fact allow you an endless number of combinations to experiment with in the tempering process. That experimentation is what led many old-time, experienced blacksmiths to the art of hardening and tempering steel. Often they claimed to have supposedly secret methods. In fact, they simply varied their procedures, always seeking ways to improve their results; through trial and error, they often succeeded.

Thus, only through each individual's experience can he find for himself — through exploration, inventiveness, discovery, and judgment — what works best for him.

The breakthrough comes when all guessing is replaced by an intuition that is a blend between feeling and knowing. As maker of tools, you are bound to experience that most gratifying of sensations: the knowledge that, while making a good tool, the probability is that the next one will be the best one yet!

CASE HARDENING STEEL

Mild steel can be hardened by heating and applying to its yellow-hot surface the purest carbon powder or a proven commercial compound. By allowing carbon to penetrate the steel at its surface only, the skin, or "casing," is hardened and thus becomes temperable. Commercial compounds can be found at machine-supply stores.

An old-fashioned case-hardening method was to pack around the steel a layer of horn-shavings (hooves of horses, cows, goats, deer — all a pure form of carbon). The whole was then wrapped in cloth. To keep oxygen out, plaster or cement, mixed with firebrick grit and reinforced with chicken wire, was cast three inches thick around the cloth-swathed bundle and left to dry thoroughly.

The whole package was then buried overnight in the glowing coals of a boiler fire in a steam-engine plant. The next day, the plaster was knocked off and the clean, dark-yellow-hot piece quenched in a drum of water. Its surface would then be brittle hard, but that hardness was only skin-deep. The advantage was that the soft core made the interior tough and resilient, while the hard surface ensured durability.

Years ago, as a student, I helped a blacksmith friend of mine case harden just such a tool in his village shop: a thirty-pound hammer head, with a "skin" that must have been all of $^1/_{16}$ of an inch deep!

THE OXIDATION COLOR SPECTRUM

The illustrations here demonstrate what happens when a bar of highly polished steel is held over a hot flame and heated gradually. The colors that appear on the surface occur during the tempering of high-carbon steels. The resulting oxidation color spectrum is a kind of temperature-color equivalency chart. In high-carbon steels, each specific color represents a specific hardness when a brittle-hard steel is being tempered over an annealing flame. (Annealing is a process whereby heated steel is cooled very slowly rather than instantly as in quenching. It "softens" most steels.)

The first color that appears in the spectrum is *faint straw*. It represents the coloration that steel takes on when it is hardest and farthest removed from the flame; *light blue* is the last color that appears in the spectrum, indicative of steel when it is softest and closest to the flame, and hottest. This color band now travels, through heat conductivity, outward until it reaches the end of the bar and disappears, leaving the previously brittle-hard bar annealed (soft). When such a high-carbon steel bar is allowed to cool slowly after heating, it leaves the steel as soft as it can become.

The six-step demonstration of what happens to a steel bar held over an annealing flame should now make clear that if you choose to quench the steel when the specific color of your choice reaches the end of the bar, that color then matches a specific hardness of the steel at the end of the bar. Thus it has been tempered, just as if you had tempered the cutting edge of a tool. Once these sequences are understood and this procedure applied to temperable scrap steels, you can proceed with confidence to temper your own tool edges.

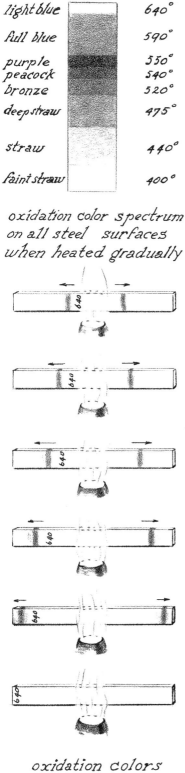

light blue	640°
full blue	590°
purple	550°
peacock	540°
bronze	520°
deep straw	475°
straw	440°
faint straw	400°

oxidation color spectrum on all steel surfaces when heated gradually

oxidation colors during heat-treating of high-carbon steel

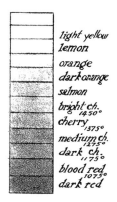

light yellow
lemon
orange
dark orange
salmon
bright ch.
 1450°
cherry
 1375°
medium ch.
 1275°
dark ch.
 1175°
blood red
 1075°
dark red

You might note that only in *brittle-hardened high-carbon steel* is the full oxidation color spectrum a graduated *hardness* indicator. Mild steel, though not temperable, will, however, show an identical oxidation color spectrum if its polished surface is heated gradually. In that situation all mild steels, regardless of a color spectrum appearance, remain soft enough to file easily.

THE COLOR RANGE OF HOT STEEL

Heat-Glow Colors

Heat-glow colors have a specific range, which the toolmaker should learn thoroughly and then determine only in the semi-dark. Much as a blacksmith constantly has to judge how hot he wants to heat steel before forging or tempering it, so must you do the same in toolmaking.

If bending the steel is all that is required, use a *yellow heat glow*. This makes steel malleable enough to bend easily. It is also a forging heat.

A *dark yellow heat glow* makes the steel a little less malleable.

A *light cherry red heat glow* (not malleable enough for forging or bending easily) is needed only when temperable steel is quenched to harden it.

A *dark cherry red heat glow* (in some temperable steels) is not quite hot enough for hardening in a direct quench.

In sum, visible heat glow relates to color and temperature, and the ability to judge these correctly is required when forging, bending, or tempering steel.

3. Making the First Tool: A Screw Driver

No matter how clearly the first steps of the very first exercises may be described — making the fire, heating the steel, hammering on the steel to shape it — the beginner must actually perform these steps himself before they become familiar. Only through practice, after repeating the steps again and again in routine sequence, will you gain the confidence that leads to competence.

This book's written and illustrated guidelines will become easier to follow because of your understanding as you read and experiment. Fewer detailed explanations will be needed since you can fill in the more obvious minute detail with which you have already become familiar.

The first lesson for the beginner is to make a screwdriver, because in this exercise, nearly every major element of toolmaking is employed with a minimum of complications.

If you are a complete novice you should first read the rules for grinding steel on motor grinders, and note all the rules on safety before beginning your first tool (see Chapter 19). Then, you may proceed with the following steps:

(1) Grinding a tapered point on the end of a rod.

From your scrap pile take a 10-inch-long engine push rod or other piece of high-carbon steel, about $5/16$ of an inch in diameter.

Grind a point, as shown, using the dry motor grinder. This point is to be the end of the screwdriver *tang,* which later will be driven into the wooden handle.

Make certain the tool rest is barely touching the rotating grinding wheel. Slide the tool back and forth as you grind, taking care not to cut grooves in the wheel. (This can happen if the sharp end of the rod is pushed hard against a single spot on the wheel face.

(2) Grinding four flat sides on the rod end.

While moving the tang back and forth, press it against the outer face of the wheel, using the tool rest to hold and steady it. Grind, without interruption, four flat surfaces to make a square cross-section, as shown.

Let the rod become as hot during sustained grinding as it can, so that the finished tang end can be forced hot into the handle. Use visegrip pliers if the rod gets too hot to hold by hand.

(3) Burning the tang into the wooden handle.

As the next step must be taken without pause, always keep a supply of standard commercial wooden file handles ready. They should have steel ferrules and be predrilled with $1/8$- to $3/16$-inch diameter, 3-inch-deep holes to guide tangs into. Note that, at a $5/16$-inch diameter, the tang is larger than the predrilled handle hole; this ensures a snug fit once tang is burned into the handle.

Quickly, while it is at its hottest, clamp the rod in the vise, tang end up. Fit the handle hole over the tang point; then tap the handle rapidly with the hammer, driving it down on the tang to its full 3-inch depth. Smoke will indicate its "burning" heat.

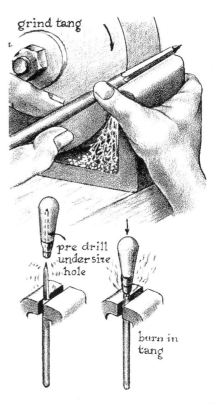

making a screwdriver

grind tang

pre drill under size hole

burn in tang

If you do these steps without interruption, the hot tang burns in evenly, without charring the wood excessively. Heated wood momentarily softens, yields, and (finally cooled) becomes hard once more. Thus, the handle will not split, is seated to perfection, and is locked against turning.

(4) Grinding and hardening the screwdriver bit.

The screwdriver bit should now be ground into a flat tapered end against the side of the wheel, as shown. As you grind the taper to knife-sharpness, you will (in a semi-dark room) begin to see a yellow heat glow appear — which is what you are after. The heat glow will "cool" to dark cherry red within one or two seconds after the tool is withdrawn from the grinding wheel. At that very moment, instantly quench it in the can of water kept alongside for that purpose.

If the resulting temper should prove to be too hard (the edge of the tool would chip in use) it means the quench has made the steel too brittle.

use the side grinder

grind bit end till cherry red & quench

polish sheen on bit end & over blue gas flame draw to bronze color & quench.

To repair, proceed as follows. Regrind the bit to an accurate taper (keeping it cool while grinding). Put a sheen on the bit end and draw to a bronze color over a gas flame, as shown.

And there you have it: a well-tempered screwdriver in about fifteen minutes! At the same time, the beginner has been introduced to the basic principles of toolmaking in the shop

Keep in mind, however, that while this simple tempering method can be applied to any small piece of steel (like a screwdriver), bigger workpieces must be heated in a forge fire to reach the necessary temperature.

4. Making a Cold Chisel and Other Simple Tools

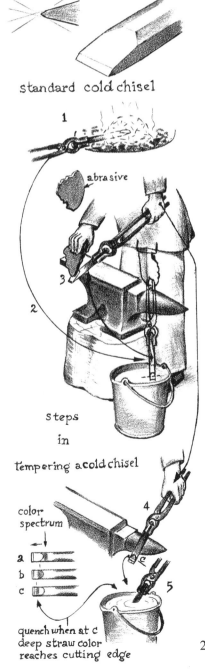

A COLD CHISEL

Select from your scrap pile a ⅝- to ⅞-inch-diameter round or octagonal bar, about 15 inches long. (As a general rule, the steel industry seems to mill much high-carbon steel into octagonal profile, though of course there are exceptions to this.)

Check, by holding the steel against the motor grinder, whether it is of high-carbon quality, as described in Chapter 2 (page 17). If in doubt, you can always resort to temperability test number 2, described in detail in Chapter 2.

SHAPING AND TEMPERING THE COLD CHISEL

(1) Shape the rod on the motor grinder, as shown, and cut off the length you want for your chisel.

(2) Build a medium-sized, clean, steady, smokeless fire.

(3) Place on the anvil, or nearby, a scrap of abrasive stone with which to put a sheen on the end of the chisel in order to judge the oxidation colors in the tempering process.

The quickest but least controlled tempering method is to hold the rod in tongs and heat about ⅜ of an inch of its end in the forge fire to a cherry red. Quench it immediately in water and test for hardness.

If you are not sure about judging the right moment at which to quench the steel, and if, in testing for hardness, you find the edge buckles or cracks, try the following, more controlled method.

Heat 1½ inches of the rod end to a dark yellow. Now, quench only ¾ of an inch of the end, as shown, and withdraw it when the visible heat glow of the rest of the steel has disappeared. This immersion step takes about ten to twenty seconds. Quickly transfer the still-hot rod to the vise or anvil and hold it firmly slanted downward over the edge. Immediately rub the end with the broken abrasive stone to make the steel shine enough to observe the oxidation colors travel through heat conductivity. Note when a dark yellow to bronze color reaches the cutting end, and at that moment quench the whole tool. This is then the right hardness for a cold chisel. (See also Chapter 2, on steel-tempering.) Whether you now harden the other end of the rod or not is optional; this is sometimes done in order to keep the steel from "cauliflowering" after long use.

In any case, cut it to the length you desire. (The average cold chisel is about 6 to 8 inches but special ones often have to be longer to cut steel in areas that are hard to get at.)

Finally, grind the bevels as shown, frequently dipping the tool in water to keep it cool during grinding so it will not lose its hardness.

standard cold chisel

1

abrasive

3

2

steps
in
tempering a cold chisel

color
spectrum

a

b

c

4

5

quench when at c
deep straw color
reaches cutting edge

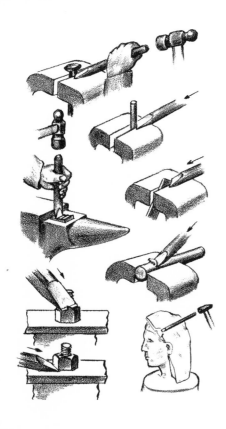

A simple cold chisel is one of the most useful tools in the shop. There are endless tasks that cannot be accomplished without this multipurpose tool, among them:

To cut off the head of a nail clamped in the vise (to make pins, rivets, nail drills, etc.).

To score a hammer-stem wedge.

To hack off a corner of a steel part.

To cut a flat section on a round rod before trueing it up with a file.

To free a nut so rust-frozen on to a bolt that no other tool will budge it. A cold chisel can notch a toehold on the edge of the nut and, with a few hard hammer blows, loosen it. A wrench can then finish the job. If all else fails to loosen a nut, then the cold chisel, placed as shown, can be driven in as a wedge, creating such enormous strain on the bolt that it will break off. By using a shearing action, in time the chisel will cut the bolt off. No matter how frustrating it often is to loosen badly rusted nuts and bolts, the cold chisel will generally solve your problem.

A small, delicate cold chisel can be used to chip plaster from waste molds in the clay-modeling and plaster-casting arts.

A CENTER PUNCH

Make a center punch out of a ½-inch-diameter high-carbon steel rod. Grind as shown. Harden just as with the cold chisel. Cut off the length desired.

A NAIL SET

Use another length of a high-carbon steel rod, previously annealed, to make a nail set. Clamp it in the vise, as shown, and use a center punch to drive a crater-type depression in its center. Now grind, as for a punch, leaving a sharp little crater in the end, and temper like a cold chisel.

CHASING TOOLS

These tools are used to texture metal surfaces (such as the surface of bronze-cast statuary) in a punching action that leaves tiny craters as well as raised portions. Chasing tools may be made with a great variety of texture patterns to suit the user. Each "business" end is tempered the same way as is a cold chisel.

PUNCHES

Sheet-metal, leather, and paper punches are made to cut through material (or indent it, as in embossing and repoussé) and to create decorative designs. These punches can also vary greatly in shape of cutting edges, according to the user's need and inventiveness. Again, they are tempered just like a cold chisel.

A PAINT MIXER

Sometimes called an agitator, this tool can be cold-bent if it is mild steel, and filed as shown. It will function well if the rod is not less than $5/16$ inch in diameter and is used at the slower rpm (on the medium pulley) of a drill press. However, if greater speed is needed or more resistant paint is to be mixed, the rod should be high-carbon steel. Such steel is inherently both stronger and more resilient in the annealed state than is mild steel.

DRILL BITS

Indispensable as accessories, drill bits can be made from leaf springs and shaped with the abrasive cutoff wheel. They can be heated, flattened, annealed, filed, and ground into their final shapes.

Temper each cutting bit a peacock or purple color to prevent it from breaking under torsion strain.

Now that you have made these simple tools, you are ready to progress to more and more complicated ones. Your confidence will increase as you work.

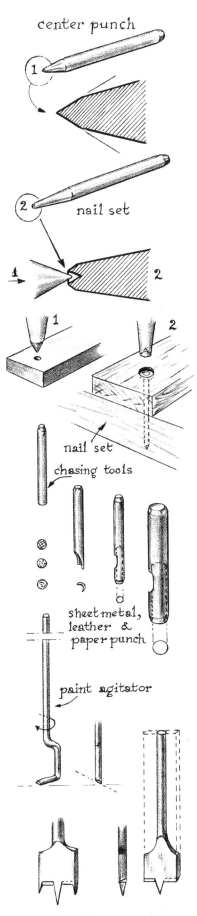

center punch

nail set

nail set

chasing tools

sheet metal, leather & paper punch

paint agitator

drill bits for wood

27

5. Making Stonecarving Tools

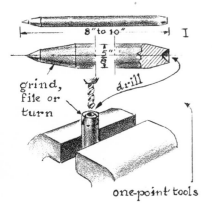

8" to 10"

grind, file or turn

drill

one-point tools

THE ONE-POINT TOOL

This stonecarving tool is simple for the beginner to make and does not need elaborate equipment. It looks like an elongated center punch and is the major tool used by sculptors working in stone. Other craftsmen use it too, for carving stone birdbaths, for chipping and fitting garden stones, and for carving other roughhewn pieces (in any stone softer than very hard granite).

Choose a ⅜- to ½-inch-diameter high-carbon steel rod (round, square, or octagonal). Test the steel with a file tip to make certain it is not too hard to cut with a hacksaw blade. Use the file *tip* only in order not to dull the file. If the file tip slides off, the stock is too hard to saw and should be annealed. (To anneal steel is to soften it. It is done simply by heating the steel to a red glow and cooling it slowly in ashes.)

Cut off an 8-inch length of the rod and grind or file its end into a point, as shown.

Heat ½ inch of this pointed end in the forge fire. As soon as a cherry red heat glow has been reached, quickly quench it in water.

Clamp the piece in the vise and test the pointed end for hardness with the file tip. If it slides off, the point is hardened. But it could be too hard: if the hardness has penetrated beyond the ½ inch at the end, the point may be too brittle. Therefore, probe with the file tip farther and farther in from the end until the file begins to grab the steel. Ideally, this should happen at ½ inch from the tip, which makes your tool just right for stonecutting. Should it occur as far in as ¾ to 1 inch, the point would be too brittle and might break off in use.

In this case, repeat every step since you first heated the tool. This time, however, the heat glow should be a little darker than cherry red before quenching. The tool tip will now be hardened correctly. The other end of the tool should be hardened in exactly the same way. (Various high-carbon steels in your scrap pile respond variably.)

Having finished this simple one-point tool, you are now well on your way to developing good judgment over the sequential steps always used in toolmaking: shaping the tool from raw stock into the tool blank; refining the blank into the final shape; hardening the tool's cutting end.

At this point, it is recommended that the beginner carefully reread the sections on tempering until all steps become thoroughly familiar. You will find that when the basic procedures are fully understood, you can work with greater ease and flexibility as you proceed to make the many tools covered in this book.

THE CLAW TOOL

The stock used for a stonecarving claw could be a ⅜- to ¾-inch-diameter high-carbon steel bar. But you may also find other usable stock: bars not less than $5/16$ of an inch thick, about 1 inch wide, and 10 inches long. Leaf springs from cars are often $5/16$ of an inch thick and of excellent steel; cut into smaller sections, one such leaf-spring blade may yield stock for a dozen or more claw blanks. Even though you find a type of scrap steel not mentioned here, it can be just as good or better, so don't hesitate to experiment with it.

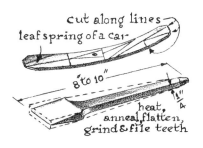

cut along lines
leaf spring of a car
8" to 10"
heat, anneal, flatten, grind & file teeth

Although an abrasive cutoff wheel can be used to cut through the leaf spring, you may prefer to have a welder do it for you with his acetylene cutting torch. In this case, all you need do is mark off with chalk the pattern of the various claws you want, just as a tailor marks off clothing patterns.

Remember, however, that any piece of high-carbon steel cut with the welder's torch is "burned" along these cuts. All burned edges have to be ground back on the motor grinder (a file would quickly dull on such hard edges) until unmarred steel is reached. The alternative to the welder's torch is the abrasive cutoff wheel (see Chapter 1, on cutting steel with an abrasive cutoff wheel), but it takes longer and assumes that you either own, or have access to, a table saw.

One end of the bar is now to be heated and flattened on the anvil with a hammer to form the shape you have chosen. The cutting end of the tool can now be annealed and the bevel either filed or ground on the motor grinder.

Clamp the beveled blank in the vise. With a triangular file (I often salvage some from a professional saw-filing shop), nick dividing marks on the edge, spacing the number of teeth you want — 5, 6, 7, 8, or more. Once you are satisfied that the division is accurate enough, cut the spaces by bearing down firmly on the file in the stroke that cuts *away* from you, idling lightly on the return stroke (so as not to dull the file any more than necessary).

File one side of the tool until the triangular grooves meet in sharp points on the tool edge; then do the other side. It is important to note that since the two outer teeth must remain as strong as those in between, that is why the blank has its two outer side facets ground as shown.

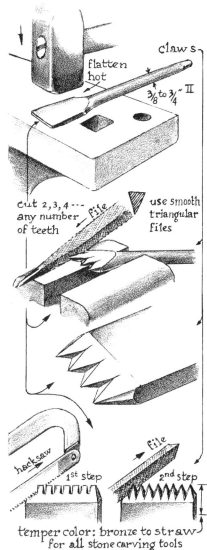

flatten hot

claws

⅜ to ¾" II

cut 2, 3, 4 --- any number of teeth

file

use smooth triangular files

hacksaw

1st step

file

2nd step

temper color: bronze to straw for all stonecarving tools

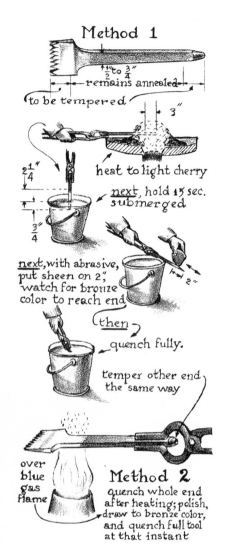

Method 1

$\frac{1}{2}$ to $\frac{3}{4}$"
—remains annealed—
(to be tempered

3"

heat to light cherry

$2\frac{1}{4}$"

next, hold 15 sec. submerged

$\frac{3}{4}$"

next, with abrasive, put sheen on 2", watch for bronze color to reach end

2"

then

quench fully.

temper other end the same way

over blue gas flame

Method 2
quench whole end after heating; polish, draw to bronze color, and quench full tool at that instant

The tool end that is struck with the hammer should be hardened just like the one-point tool. But the delicate teeth of the claw require a more cautious tempering method, which can be accomplished in one of two ways:

(1) In the forge fire, heat 2¼ inches of the claw end to a light cherry glow. Quench by immersing only the final ¾ inch in the water, just long enough (about fifteen seconds) to see the heat glow disappear in the unsubmerged part. At that moment, quickly withdraw the tool and place it over the edge of the bucket. Rub it with a piece of sandstone or scrap of abrasive stone, creating a bright metallic sheen on the ¾-inch quenched end. The heat stored in the tool will now reheat the file-hard quenched end through conductivity. First, a light straw color will appear, but as the stored heat travels on, the teeth become hotter and hotter and light straw yellow turns to dark straw yellow, and next to bronze.

At this moment, quench the whole tool, to arrest the tempering process; this ensures that the teeth are now of a hardness to cut fairly hard stone, yet not so brittle that they might break off.

(2) This tempering method is similar to the first but gives you more control. This time, when 1 inch of the cutting end is heated to light cherry red, *quench the whole tool.*

Once the tool has cooled, polish the claw end with an abrasive stone or carborundum paper to a mirror sheen. Now use a blue flame (from a propane gas torch) to reheat the steel, thus drawing the temper colors. Watch the oxidation colors run their sequence as heat is conducted toward the claw end. Just as this color band can be arrested by full quenching, so can it be retarded by moving the tool farther from the heat source. When the teeth are drawn from a dark straw yellow to bronze, quench the tool once more.

This controlled method is always preferable when tempering an important or delicate tool.

THE BUSH TOOL

This tool with a serrated face is often referred to as a "nine-point." The bush tool actually crushes the stone, pulverizing its outer surface, whereas one-points and claws *chip* stone. The bush tool requires a steel stock about 1½ inches in diameter or square cross-section. Such heavy stock may be cut from a salvaged car axle, as shown.

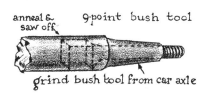

anneal & saw off   9-point bush tool

grind bush tool from car axle

When filing the teeth of a bush tool, make certain, as with the claw, that the steel is annealed by burying the heated tool end in ashes to cool the steel very slowly. This makes high-carbon steel as soft as it will ever get — sufficiently softer than files used on it, which otherwise would become dull quickly.

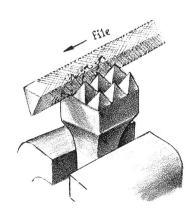

file

Once you are satisfied that the steel is properly annealed, clamp the tool blank vertically in the vise, as shown. First, prepare the teeth locations with a hacksaw. Follow up with a triangular file; and, finally, file the side facets on each tooth by slanting the file, as demonstrated in enlarged detail.

Once ground and filed, the points should be tempered as suggested in the first method for claw-tempering. This time, however, draw temper color to light straw yellow (harder than dark straw yellow). The reason is that the bush points will not be unduly strained by side tension, and thus can take a harder temper for longer wear.

Bush tools of a smaller caliber may be made from heavy-gauge coil springs. These are often to be found as scrap steel from heavy trucks. When a section of such a coil is cut on the abrasive cutoff wheel and heated and straightened, it will be long enough to make many sturdy stonecarving tools. The diameter of this steel is rarely over ¾ inch, just enough to file into its end-face a series of small points for a bush tool used to texture the delicate detail of stone sculptures.

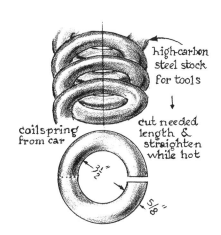

high-carbon steel stock for tools

cut needed length & straighten while hot

coilspring from car

6. Sharpening Tools

Sharpening tools should be done on machine grinders if your shop is equipped for it, as power grinders not only save time and effort but result in a more perfect cutting edge as well. Sharpening tools on hand stones, although described at the end of this chapter, will prove your second choice once both methods have become familiar. You may then join me in saying, "Throw all hand stones out of the window" if machine grinders and buffers are available.

MAKING A SIDE GRINDER

The materials needed to build this power grinder are: a ¼ hp electric motor, scrap plywood, a salvaged abrasive cutoff wheel disc, setscrews, and some wood glue.

Cut out one ½-inch-thick plywood circle, about 10 inches in diameter (approximately the size of the salvaged abrasive cutoff wheel), and one ½-inch thick about 6 inches in diameter.

Also cut two that are 3 inches in diameter. Glue all four plywood pieces together, concentrically, between wood clamps.

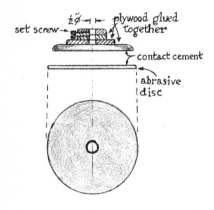

Next, drill a ½-inch-diameter hole in the exact center of this assembly to receive the ½-inch-diameter shaft of a standard ¼ hp electric motor.

To secure this assembly on the shaft, the wooden hub part should accommodate a ⅜-inch-diameter wood screw as a "setscrew." Drill a ¼-inch-diameter hole in the hub, as shown (you can make the drill from a ¼-inch-diameter mild-steel rod 7 inches long, its end filed to resemble a drill tip). Then, forcibly screw a ⅜-inch wood screw, its threads rubbed in candle wax, into this undersized hole.

The motor shaft, as a rule, will have a key slot or flattened facet on to which the setscrew can lock. If not, drill a shallow hole into the shaft at a measured distance from its end, to seat the setscrew firmly.

Thus anchored to the motor shaft, the wood disc assembly can now operate as a wood lathe. An improvised tool rest, as shown, will assist your lathe-cutting.

When you are satisfied that the disc is perfectly flat and round (check with a straightedge), remove the assembly and apply contact cement to both the face of the wood disc and one side of the abrasive cutoff wheel. Once this cement has become dry enough (in a minute or so), press the two together. (A good way is to place the assembly flat on the floor, cutoff wheel down, and step on the hub, using your body weight to press the two cemented areas together.)

The next step is to remove the plastic coating from the face of the cutoff wheel so that the grit is entirely exposed. For this purpose, a piece of flat concrete, such as broken pieces of sidewalk or cement waste from building projects, is useful.

Place the cement slab horizontally, as shown, so that the abrasive disc can be moved over it in a grinding action. Sprinkle the slab constantly with coarse sand and a plentiful supply of water. The downward pressure will grind off the plastic, exposing the grit on the cutoff disc.

Finally, lock the finished assembly on to the motor shaft: you now have made one of the most useful machine tools in your shop — a side grinder.

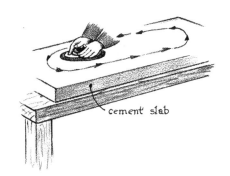

cement slab

USE OF THE SIDE GRINDER

The advantages of a single-purpose side grinder over standard multi-purpose grinding wheels are obvious. Because of the accessibility of the disc surface, you have a full, uninterrupted view when grinding specific bevel angles, cone shapes on blades, flat surfaces on long chisels and knives, as well as the small, flat facets required in V-shaped gouge uprights.

In short, all flat tool surfaces can now be safely and conveniently ground. The composition of this cutoff wheel is so hard and durable that I have found it to outlast every other stone for grinding purposes.

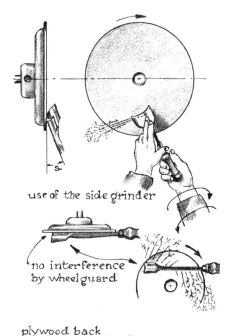

use of the side grinder

no interference by wheelguard

plywood back

thin wheel

Salvaging Worn Stones

When grinding wheels become worn down and thin, and side pressure would endanger their brittle structure to the point of breakage (a break would make them then fly apart), they must be reinforced. Fit a standard extension shaft and cup washer precisely against the shoulder of the motor extension. Between this washer and the thin stone, place a disc of plywood that is 1 inch thick and 1 inch larger in diameter than the worn stone. The side pressure will thus be absorbed by the plywood backing during grinding.

Anchor your now salvaged grinding unit to the shaft with washer and nut; the stone will serve well, though the washer and nut somewhat reduce the total usable surface of the stone.

As a double precaution, a protective wood ring can be nailed or glued on to the backing disc; or, the stone itself can be glued to the disc.

The Dressing Tool

A dressing tool is used to repair worn grinding wheels by smoothing out grooves and cleaning off dirt. The toothed wheels of the dresser are strung on a shaft smaller than the wheels' holes, causing them to spin independently and "rattle" against the revolving grinding wheel. This "rattling" action results in hammer-like blows that break down high spots on the stone's spinning surface.

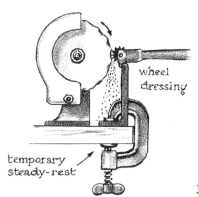

wheel dressing

temporary steady-rest

Dressing Worn Grinding Wheels

Dress a worn stone by adjusting the tool rest (which normally almost touches the stone) so that it is parallel to the stone. It must be far enough away to allow the dresser toe to hook over the edge of the tool rest, yet close enough so that the dresser wheels barely touch the stone's high spots. Then start the motor and move the dresser along the tool rest, wearing down the wheel. An important precaution to take during this operation is to use a nose mask and goggles. Goggles are essential because of the danger of flying sparks and stone particles. But the mask will not be necessary if you breathe properly: inhale deeply before starting the action, hold your breath while the dresser is cutting; exhale when the dresser stops cutting. Let dust settle, and repeat.

If the stone's surface is not sufficiently cleaned in the first operation, tap the tool rest lightly with a hammer to bring it a little closer to the stone. Each such readjustment permits the stone to be better dressed and, in time, the surface will be dressed with great accuracy.

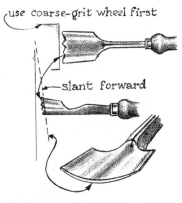

use coarse-grit wheel first

slant forward

Dressing a Broken Gouge Edge

In dressing a wood gouge, be sure to cool its edge frequently with water to prevent the hard steel from losing its temper on the coarse, hard stone of the grinder.

Slant the blade against the stone at the angle originally designed for it. (See Chapter 12, on wood-gouge design.) This slanted edge can be accurately aligned on the side grinder. The slight burr that forms must be scraped off the edge.

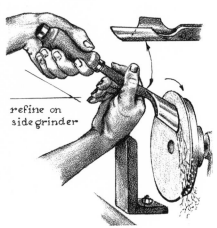

refine on
side grinder

You are now ready to grind the beveled edge of the tool on the various grinders. Take extra care against loss of temper, because the thinner the steel becomes, the sooner heat accumulates. To prevent it, more frequent cooling and slower grinding with less pressure are necessary.

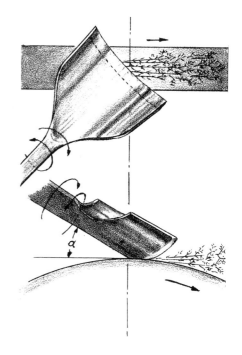

The mirror-like reflection seen on the re-dressed edge must be watched during bevel grinding. That reflection guides you in maintaining an even and gradual approach of the outside bevel plane to the inside blade plane.

With continued grinding, the last little "sheen" will eventually disappear. This is the sign that the outside bevel and the inside plane of the blade have met, creating a minute burr, indicating that no further grinding is needed.

Refine the texture of the ground surface of the bevel on the rubber abrasive wheel and, finally, finish on the tripoli-treated buffer. This will sharpen your wood gouge to perfection.

THE RUBBER ABRASIVE WHEEL

The rubber abrasive wheel is used for honing tools after they have been sharpened on stones. Such wheels are very tricky to work with, but their advantages are great. Because rubber is inherently softer than stone, sharpened steel has a tendency to bite into — sometimes actually bite a hunk *out* of — the spinning rubber grinder. Such an accident can give one an expensive scare, since rubber abrasive wheels are costly. Nevertheless, it is worthwhile learning to use this tool *safely* so that you may enjoy its many benefits. It works much faster than honing by hand. To hand-hone a tool edge to a refined texture takes at least ten to twenty minutes; an abrasive rubber wheel produces an identical, or even smoother, result in ten to twenty seconds.

No wonder this modern honing method is a blessing. For instance, I can quickly prepare a dozen or more woodcarving gouges to start the day's carving by honing their edges on the rubber abrasive wheel, then adding a final finish on the buffing wheel. Such tool edges need no further honing or stropping on the buffer for days on end, even when one is using the tools uninterruptedly on clean wood of various hardnesses.

These two wheels — the rubber abrasive wheel and the cotton buffing wheel (treated with tripoli compound) — will prove indispensable in your shop.

If you have never used a rubber wheel before, I suggest you take a sharp-pointed thin wire or a common pin and touch its point to the rotating wheel lightly, as shown, to experience which angle is the safest between wheel and thin probe. In position 1, it grabs somewhat; in position 3, the probe is grabbed strongly; in position 2, the probe seems to stay on the spinning surface as if sliding over it (which is safe). Now, try to imagine how a razor-sharp tool would behave if pressed on the rubber wheel in any save one of these three tool positions:

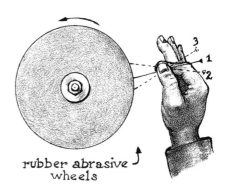

rubber abrasive wheels

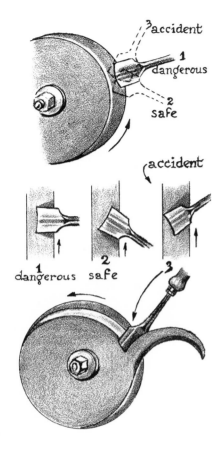

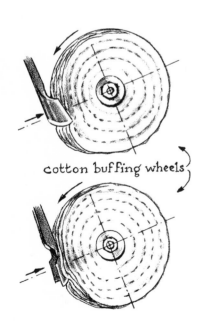

cotton buffing wheels

Position 1 is dangerous because any slight change of angle between tool edge and oncoming rubber surface will cause the tool to bite into the wheel. The soft rubber must slide under the steel edge unimpeded, to avoid accident.

Position 3 shows the sharp edge actually biting into the wheel. A strip of rubber is sliced off and the wheel thus badly damaged.

Position 2 is safe, as shown, because the whole tool bevel, in rocking motion, is pressed on the surface in the same direction that the wheel revolves. This ensures that the tool will not be "going against the grain."

Once in a while, the surface of the rubber becomes shiny with metal pulp, which reduces the effectiveness of its honing action. To clean the rubber, hold the sharp end of a broad flat file very firmly at a right angle to the surface of the wheel rim. This breaks through the outer rubber layer slightly, exposing a fresh, unused surface. As with all abrasive wheels, avoid breathing the pulp dust that is thrown off.

Rubber abrasive wheels are expensive, but should you accidentally slice a chunk out of one, it can be salvaged. Dismount the wheel and lay it on your workbench or the end of a wood stump. Cut off the uneven surface on the outside of the wheel with a chisel. After this new, smaller diameter has been cut, remount the wheel and use a file to refine it, with a scraping-cutting action, as was done in cleaning the metal residue from the wheel rim.

If more serious slicing occurs (perhaps by a heavy tool such as an ax), don't throw away the wheel remnants. Salvage any little portions, and cut them into discs of various diameters. These pieces can now be drilled through their centers (with a sharpened little tube) to receive stove-bolt arbors and washers. Such units will then serve excellently to refine the insides of your various woodcarving gouges. (Such gouges require smooth and even surfaces so that wood chips will slide off easily.)

The rubber abrasive wheel may give you a scare if there is an accident. But, handled with care, it will prove irresistibly useful daily for honing cutting tools.

THE BUFFING WHEEL

After honing, tools are finally refined by polishing on the buffing wheel. Buffing a steel surface is actually polishing it to an even finer texture than that left by the finest-grit grinding wheels and rubber abrasive wheels.

Besides putting on a sheen for appearance's sake, buffing is the absolutely essential final step in mechanical tool sharpening. The cutting edge is mechanically stropped on the buffer much as a razor blade is hand-stropped on leather. The tool, held tangentially to the buffer rim and pressed into it (first the tool's front, then its back), thus receives its finished edge.

Press a block of buffing compound on the rim of the fast-spinning cotton buffing wheel. This abrasive will momentarily melt, with the heat created by the spinning wheel, and adhere to it, transforming the cotton into the finest abrasive surface. I find that, for the buffing of steel, tripoli compound in its coarsest grit works quickly, yet is fine enough. During buffing action the wax-held granules are gradually flung off the wheel, so more compound must be added repeatedly.

Big industries, such as industrial plating companies, naturally have leftover pieces of buffing compound for which they have no further use. As such waste generally ends in the scrap bin, such shops are usually quite generous once their interest and sympathy are aroused by the work of the artist-hobbyist.

Some years ago, I stepped into the office of one of those plating companies. Showing the foreman some of my fine woodcarving tools, and some photographs of my stone and wood sculptures, I explained my need for buffing compound remnants. The boss took one look at my work and led me directly to a thirty-gallon scrap barrel full of fist-sized blocks of tripoli compound!

In industry, these pieces begin as large rectangular blocks, 10 inches long and 2½ by 1½ inches in cross-section. When they are hand-held against fast-spinning, 20-inch-diameter buffing wheels, the blocks wear rapidly and soon become too small to handle with ease.

The foreman urged me to help myself to these discards (especially since I had given him a picture of one of my sculptures!). He filled a large paper bag with about twenty pounds of those remnants, and for many years I was supplied — free — with the very best of buffing compounds.

USE OF HAND STONES

Tool-sharpening by hand requires the use, in sequence, of: one double-grit carborundum stone, one honing stone, one leather strop with emery powder, and thin oil or kerosene.

If an extremely dull chisel (or one that has been badly nicked) is to be sharpened, a coarse-grit stone must be used first, for quantity steel-removal. But if an only slightly dull chisel is to be sharpened, then begin with a fine-grit stone, and follow up by honing and stropping.

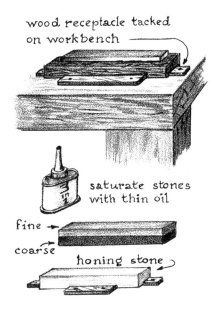

wood receptacle tacked on workbench

saturate stones with thin oil

fine →
coarse →

honing stone

Submerge a double-grit (one side coarse, the other, fine) carborundum stone in thin oil until it is saturated. (The standard household brand, 3-in-One oil, will do fine and is available everywhere.) Carborundum stones absorb oil like a sponge, and still more oil must be added to act as a flushing agent to carry off the ground metal during tool-sharpening. The excess oil thus keeps the stone's pores open and its cutting granules exposed to the steel. (Kerosene, instead of thin oil, will also do.) Cradle the stone in some sheet steel or aluminum foil, leaving the top exposed, to keep the oil from draining out. Then, in order to have both hands free to handle the tool, clamp the stone to your workbench (or on a block of wood in your vise) with four little wood cleats, as shown.

Keep in mind that a dry, unsoaked stone will only cause the ground steel particles to clog up the stone's open pores, rendering it, in due time, completely ineffective. Therefore, keep flushing the steel pulp with oil, from time to time. Use additional oil and a small rag to wipe the steel-pulp-laden oil off before adding fresh oil. These are good habits to practice when hand-sharpening tools. (Incidentally, if the stone is of a type where water is recommended as a cutting liquid, the same procedure holds true.)

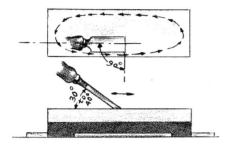

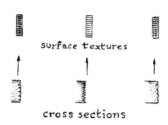

surface textures

cross sections

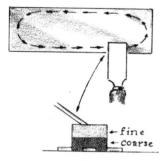

← fine
← coarse

SHARPENING A CARPENTER'S CHISEL

Grinding Motions

A carpenter's chisel, or wood chisel, has two angles, both of which must concern you: the 30° to 40° angle of the cutting bevel; and the 90° angle, at which the chisel itself is held (see illustration). Therefore, you must sharpen the bevel without changing its correct angle, while at the same time maintaining the 90° angle of the edge to the length of the chisel. Only practice will give you the necessary skill to move the chisel over the stone evenly while maintaining both angles.

If you rock the chisel up and down while sharpening it, the bevel will become rounded instead of flat: a rounded bevel tends to make the tool jump out of any wood you try to cut, whereas a flat bevel keeps the tool steady as it is manipulated.

If you bear down on the chisel more on one side or the other, you will in time affect the 90° angle of the edge to the length of the chisel.

Assuming, now, that you are holding the chisel steady, and correctly (both angles unvarying during the grinding), the movement ought to be elliptical, as shown.

An elliptical movement continually "crosscuts" the tiny grooves ground into the steel surface, whereas a straight back-and-forth movement grinds the grooves straight. The crosscut texture produced by elliptical grinding cuts the steel faster, while, at the same time, leaving a finer texture on the tool. A straight back-and-forth movement, however, cuts the steel more slowly, since grit slides continually in the same grooves, leaving a coarser texture.

In any case, whether you use elliptical or straight movements, try to utilize as much of the stone's surface as possible, to avoid wearing deep grooves in it. Should it become worn or grooved, resurface it with the same method you use in re-dressing the side grinder (see page 33).

To summarize: Press the tool steadily downward, move it elliptically, and always at the correct angle. Use as much of the stone's surface as possible, so that no local wear hollows out the stone too fast; remember to add oil from time to time; and wipe off steel pulp before each fresh oiling.

Honing the Burr

Grind the tool bevel down on the coarse-grit side of the stone until it meets the other side of the blade at its edge; then turn the stone and continue grinding on the fine-grit side until an almost imperceptible, fine burr forms. Do *not* attempt to remove the burr yet. The burr is so thin that it will bend away from the stone, instead of being ground off. A correctly tempered chisel produces a springlike burr. (Never grind the *flat* side of the chisel in an attempt to grind off the burr.) If the tool edge of a delicate wood gouge or chisel should not form a burr, it simply means that the steel was tempered too hard, making the burr crack off during grinding, instead of bending. This leaves a microscopic jagged edge which will scratch the surface of soft wood, and break on hard wood.

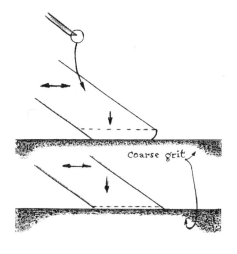

Any further grinding of the burr will only lengthen it, while reducing the life span of the tool needlessly. So turn, now, to the honing stone to refine the texture of the bevel surface. Use thin oil or water as a flushing agent, and hone until the bevel becomes mirror-smooth. When the entire bevel surface shows the honing stone's texture, the burr should still be there.

Stropping the Burr

It is now time to remove the burr. Fix a strip of leather on a piece of flat wood, then clamp it in your vise or to your workbench. This leather strop should now be oiled a little and sprinkled with some extra-fine emery dust.

Just as a barber strops an old-fashioned razor on a leather strop, draw the tool's edge backward over the leather as shown — first one side, then the other — pressing the tool flush with each stroke.

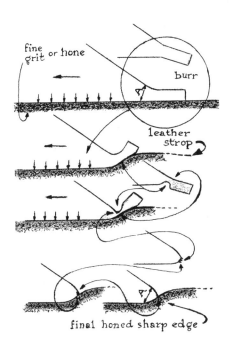

In due time, the emery dust held by the leather and oil will wear the burr so thin that metal fatigue finally makes it crack off, like a tin-can lid bent back and forth.

Now, only a minute, saw-toothed edge remains. Continue stropping *after* the burr has come off, so as to wear this jagged edge down to a microscopically smooth, rounded edge. This achieves an ideal cutting edge, and one that, because it is too tough to bend, is also extremely durable.

Since the grinding effect of the strop deals with a microscopic thickness of steel, it ensures an edge that will remain sharp enough to need only occasional stropping. The life of the tool is thus prolonged, since the harsher grinding on stones will not be needed for some time.

You may now recognize that the foregoing explanation is a welcome answer to that persistent, nagging question: What is the best way to sharpen a tool? Judging from my own long-time experience, the method I have developed and offer here is the best, since it results in the ideal cutting edge and is accomplished in seconds, instead of hours, thanks to power tools and a better understanding of what is involved.

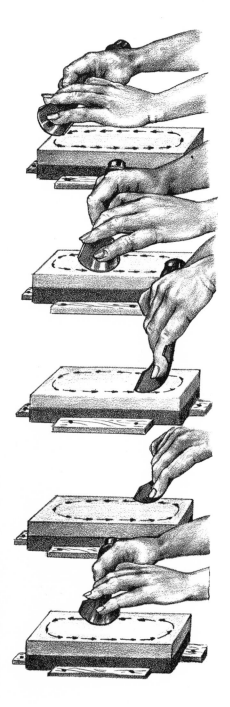

SHARPENING ROUND GOUGES

Like wood chisels, round gouges should be ground in elliptical movements, in a continuous cycle of tool and hand over stone. As shown, the left hand guides the blade end while the right hand rotates the tool around its lengthwise axis. This rotation creates the rocking movement of the blade, while both hands aim to maintain the angle of the tool bevel.

Remember that while some tools may be moved in a rotary action during grinding, their cutting facets must remain flat, in order not to "jump out" of the wood. The tool then would fight your hand instead of obeying it under easy guidance.

USE OF THE DRY GRINDER

⅓ to ½ hp electric dry grinder

Most tools in your shop can be ground on a standard ¼ hp 1750 rpm motor grinder with two wheels (one coarse-grit, the other fine.)

The tool rest, preferably bolted to your workbench, is adjusted simply by tapping it with a hammer to close the gap between tool rest and stone. A can of water to cool the tool should hang between the two wheels, so that instant quenching is possible should the tool edge become too hot to touch.

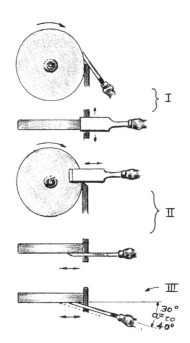

In sharpening a flat carpenter's chisel, for example, hold the blade at the correct angle to the wheel; then move the chisel back and forth over the wheel-rim surface, while maintaining the angle. This back-and-forth movement is corrective: it tends to keep an initially accurately dressed wheel aligned, and makes a *less* accurate wheel *more* accurate. If the wheel should be badly grooved, first re-dress it.

Should a badly abused tool come into your possession, first refine the *flat side* of the chisel on the side of the wheel, or on the side grinder. Do not grind the bevel until a flat surface has been restored.

Grinding new bevels can be tricky, and if, somehow, they turn out less than perfect, a gentle and careful touch-up of the bevel facet on the side of the wheel may save the day. Avoid, however, using the wheel's side if there is a reasonable chance that the wheel's rim can do the job. It is far more difficult to repair a groove in a wheel's side than on its rim.

testing for sharpness

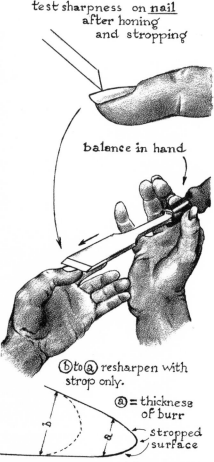

right
way to detect burr

wrong
way

lightly feel for first sign of burr
after sharpening on stones
__next:__

test sharpness on __nail__
after honing
and stropping

balance in hand

ⓑ to ⓐ resharpen with
strop only.

ⓐ = thickness
of burr

stropped
surface

microscopic view of final edge
anything thinner than ⓐ will
bend or break, no matter how
perfect the temper

TESTING FOR SHARPNESS

Lightly touch the flat side of a tool blade with your finger, drawing your finger over the edge, as shown. If a burr has formed at the cutting edge, you will feel it instantly, even if you cannot see it without a magnifying glass.

You cannot tell if a burr has formed if you scrape or rub your finger *across* the tool edge.

Running your finger *along* the edge also is not satisfactory because you are likely to cut yourself. Burrs are razor sharp, with jagged edges.

Once you have established that a slight burr has formed evenly over the whole tool edge, strop it off, as described earlier. The only test now left is that for sharpness.

If the tool edge, gently placed on the fingernail, as shown, seems to "pick" at the nail, rather than slide off, that particular spot of the tool edge is sharp. Any part of the edge that slides off the nail needs further sharpening. Grind, hone, and strop until the edge "picks" at your nail at every local spot along its entire width (while the tool is balanced in your other hand at a barely "cutting" slant). Your tool is now truly sharp.

Note from the enlarged microscopic diagram of an ideally sharp tool that the edge is actually *rounded*.

7. Making Carpenter's Chisels

THE NARROW CHISEL

From your scrap pile, select a leaf spring of a car as stock for a flat, one-inch chisel. Heat one foot of it to a dark yellow in the forge, straighten the curve on the anvil, then let it cool slowly in ashes. This anneals the steel so that it can be cut with a hacksaw and filed without damaging saw or file.

Suppose the leaf spring is 2½ inches wide by ¼ inch thick, and that you want a 1-inch-wide chisel. Saw the spring lengthwise. (One blank will be 1 inch wide, the other 1⅜ inches, with a ⅛-inch loss in saw cut; the wider piece can be saved for future use.)

Scribe the exact outline of the chisel on the blank, allowing for a 3½-inch tang. Cut out the blank by filing or grinding along this outline.

If the blade is thicker than you wish, file it down gradually, tapering toward the cutting edge. Use the side grinder if you prefer. Refine the surface with progressively finer grits on small rubber-backed abrasive discs. Finish up on the buffer for a final mirror-smoothness.

Next, grind the cutting-edge bevel at an angle of approximately 30°. Finally, temper the tool and burn the tang into the handle as described in Chapter 10.

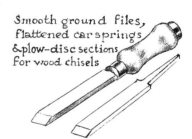

Smooth ground files, flattened car springs & plow-disc sections for wood chisels

THE BROAD-BLADE CHISEL

A wide chisel is made in the same way as a narrow chisel, with one exception: any blade broader than 2 inches must be brittle-quenched in *oil* instead of water, to avoid or minimize the chance of warping. You will doubtless have to experiment (holding the blade on the vertical, horizontal, or diagonal during quenching) before you find the best way to maintain its straight edge.

The next step is to clean and polish the blade mirror-smooth in order to draw its temper color. Here, especially, with a wide blade, you must be extremely careful to prevent warping during reheating over the annealing flame. Aim for a slow, even drawing of oxidation color over the full blade.

Once the desired temper color has been reached, immediately withdraw the blade from the flame and cool it slowly at room temperature. The tension developed during the initial brittle-quenching will be released by this slow cooling process, thus strengthening the blade overall.

Caution must also be exercised when sharpening broad-bladed chisels. It is best to let them cool slowly from time to time, as you sharpen. Or, if you grind slowly enough, the blade will be cooled by the air that is centrifugally blown along the wheel rim as you work. Don't attempt to cool the blade during grinding by quenching it in water, for that, too, can warp it.

files must be
ground smooth
before shaping them
into tools

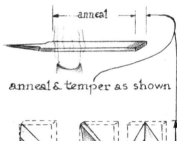

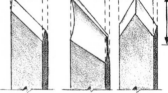

anneal & temper as shown

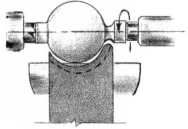

wood lathe-turning tools
made from old files

leafsprings ground into
special profiles for turning

FILES AS STOCK FOR CHISELS AND LATHE-TURNING TOOLS

Old flat files lend themselves excellently to making flat chisels (and lathe-turning tools) because the carbon content of files is much higher than that of spring steel.

First, be sure to grind the old file clean of all traces of corrugations, because any remaining grooves can cause the steel to "crack" during quenching in the tempering process (the same principle as cracking glass with a glass cutter).

During grinding, do not lose the file's brittle hardness through overheating (the color *blue* would appear). Assuming that the steel has not lost its hardness, the cutting end can now be drawn a dark bronze to peacock color for a hard cutting edge. The remainder of the tool should be annealed, and the tang heated and burned into the handle.

Finish the chisel by grinding and sharpening a beveled edge, taking great care not to overheat and so anneal it.

The variously shaped cutting ends of lathe-turning tools, which can also be made from old files, ground clean, may be drawn to a straw yellow, if the steel is not thinner than ¼ inch. Anneal the remainder.

If leaf springs of cars are used, choose a section 2 inches wide and cut it 18 inches long. The cutting ends may be ground (be careful not to lose hardness by overheating during grinding) and shaped into various profiles for special wood-turning projects. No handle is needed on such 18-inch-long tools. Turning a wood sphere, as shown, is a one-movement operation.

I have many sections of car leaf springs (most retain the original slight spring curve) whose ends have been ground into various profiles useful for cutting lathe-turned curves in woods.

8. Making Cutting Tools

KNIFE FOR CARDBOARD AND PAPER

A small cutting knife is invaluable when you are working with cardboard and paper. It can be used to make all sorts of articles: boxes, mobiles, art constructions, commercial displays and decorations, mats for watercolors, prints, photographs, and the like.

This tool's design grew out of a Swedish system of manual training called *sloyd*. Taught in many Scandinavian countries, the sloyd-knife art extends to a variety of cardboard and woodcarving crafts. The knife shown here is designed especially to fit the hand as you bear down on the tool during cutting.

There are many kinds of scrap steel suitable as stock for this sloyd knife (as well as for many other cutting tools). The following are suggested: heavy-gauge industrial hacksaw blades, discarded lawn-mower blades, industrial band and circular-saw blades, old butcher knives or cleavers, and — since the advent of the power chain saw — old handsaws, which are often found either secondhand or abandoned around farmyards or barns. All such steel is high-carbon, hard-tempered, and therefore highly suitable for cutting tools.

Step 1. Cut the blank, as shown, on your abrasive cutoff wheel. *Keep the steel cool*, in order to preserve its hardened state, frequently quenching in water, particularly the part intended for the knife blade.

Step 2. The wooden pieces of the handle will be attached to the steel with rivets, but first the two holes in the steel must be carefully prepared. On hard-tempered steel, your drill will be ruined in short order, so the spots where the holes will be drilled must be annealed.

Mark off the two locations on the blade. Now, make a simple mild-steel drill from a nail by cutting off its head and grinding its end flat, as shown. Put it in the drill press, and at *high* speed, press this drill on your hole mark until the friction heats the spot. When it turns blue, it is annealed. Do the same for the second hole mark.

Step 3. Next, use a high-speed-steel twist drill (the size of the rivets you plan to use), but run it at *slow* speed. It should have no difficulty in cutting through the annealed area to make the holes.

Step 4. Choose a piece of hardwood for the handle, selecting whichever grain or color suits your taste. Cut two pieces, a little larger than the desired handle size.

The two holes in the steel can be marked off on each wood piece and drilled. To seat the washer in the handle, drill a slight depression with a blunt-ended bit, the diameter of the washer, or rout-countersink in the wood.

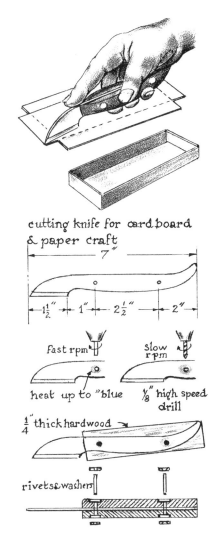

cutting knife for cardboard & paper craft

7"

1½"   1"   2½"   2"

fast rpm   slow rpm

heat up to "blue"   ⅛" high speed drill

¼" thick hardwood

rivets & washers

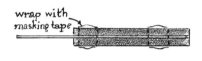

wrap with masking tape

Next, rivet the wood sections on to the metal handle with small brass or steel washers that have countersunk holes. You can countersink the washers on the drill press (using a regular large drill) by holding them in visegrip pliers. A quicker way is to put the washer on a hardwood stump and hammer it once with a blunt center punch. This will spread the washer hole into a little conical depression wide enough to fit the rivet head.

If you have no flatheaded store rivets on hand, improvise by clipping off nails to a size that will fit the holes snugly. Clipped sections of brass welding rod will do as well. Allow a little excess length, to form the rivet heads.

Step 5. After inserting rivet sections into washers, and washers into the wood-steel-wood handle assembly, tape it all together with masking tape and place it on your anvil.

Strike the rivet first with the flat side of a lightweight ball-peen hammer. The mild steel spreads outward as you hammer, forming a little burr edge, which now begins to act as a rivet head so that you can turn the knife handle over without the washer dropping out. The other end of the rivet, backed by the hard anvil, will also have been compacted and spread somewhat.

Hammering with ball-peen and flat face alternately on both sides of the handle, the forming rivet heads soon fill the washers' countersinks completely, leaving little to be trimmed off.

Step 6. Using either a rasp, a flexible rubber-backed sanding disc, or a chisel, trim all excess wood and shape the handle, as shown. Hold it against your side grinder so that the rivet heads can be ground flush with the wood. Take care not to grind the heads more than necessary, leaving enough to secure the handle assembly.

Refine and polish the wood finish as described in Chapter 10.

trim excesswood & polish

A CHERRY PITTER

This all-purpose kitchen tool can also be used to pick out the eyes of potatoes and pineapples after they have been peeled, to remove small seeds and bad spots in almost any fruit or vegetable, and to form fruits, such as melon balls, for fancy desserts. This tool cuts by rotating around its axis in a scooping motion.

A ⅜-inch-diameter straightened coil spring can be used for stock. Cut a 14-inch length so that it can be comfortably hand-held while its cutting end is heated to a yellow glow in the fire. Place the hot tip of the rod on the polished, rounded, and tempered end of a ¾-inch-diameter bar that you have previously clamped in the vise to serve as a saddle. Pound the hot tip over this saddle with a 1½-pound hammer until you judge that the "spoon" that has formed is only $1/16$ inch thick in the center.

Shape the spoon on the motor grinder so that the blade gradually thins out to razor-sharpness at its edge.

Grind a round shank, $3/16$ of an inch in diameter and 2 inches long, followed by a 1½-inch tang, which should be square and tapered.

Temper the blade to the hardness indicated by a straw yellow oxidation color, and burn the tang into its handle as described in Chapter 12. Finally, buff the entire blade to a smooth and sharp finish on your cotton buffing wheel.

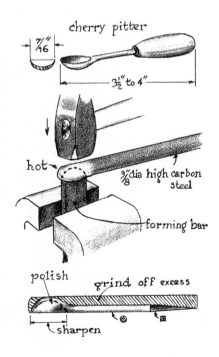

cherry pitter

$\frac{7}{16}''$

3½" to 4"

hot

⅜"dia high carbon steel

forming bar

polish

grind off excess

sharpen

GARDEN TOOLS

The fishhook-like tool is designed to cut plant roots. By forcing it down into the earth next to the root, the hook, which is sharpened on the inside, cuts the root on the up stroke.

Use a piece of a car bumper as stock. This steel is of high-carbon quality and should be about $1/8$ to $3/16$ of an inch thick.

Scribe the pattern of the blade on a properly annealed and flattened section. Drill the two holes where the rivets will attach the two wooden pieces to the handle.

Next, sharpen and temper the whole blade a peacock color and rivet the wood pieces, as with the sloyd knife handle.

If you prefer, you can seat the tool in a one-piece wooden handle. In that case, the tang should be ground to a slight taper, then heated and burned into the handle, as is done with woodcarving tools (see Chapter 10). Leave a $1/8$-inch space between handle and tool-shank shoulder and let the whole unit cool somewhat; then drive the handle down flush with the shoulder. This still warm, yet resilient, wood grasps the tapered tang and, once fully cooled, locks in securely.

In tools such as these, which exert a pulling rather than pushing action, tangs should extend a little beyond the wood handles; the $1/8$ to $1/4$ inch of steel that protrudes can then be hooked over the end, locking handle and blade together permanently.

Try to avoid accidental overheating during grinding since it might require retempering the knife blade. If this does become necessary, be careful, if the handle is already attached, that the wood does not overheat and scorch. To prevent this, bind the handle with a soaking-wet cloth and thin wire.

Tempering procedures for garden tools will vary according to the amount of stress you expect a given tool to undergo. For example, to ensure resilience at a location apt to break under heavy strain (where handle and blade meet), anneal such areas locally or else temper the steel to purple to avoid brittleness.

The *harvesting tool*, which cuts with a downward stroke, is useful in harvesting thick-rooted vegetables like lettuce, cabbage, and asparagus. It is easily made from a scrap industrial hacksaw blade. Make the wooden handle as for the fishhook tool, and grind the steel blade cautiously so that it does not lose its temper.

A small, narrow *scoop shovel*, useful in transplanting seedlings, can be made from an old handsaw. Cut the section desired with your abrasive cutoff wheel. Next, heat the shank and tang portion to a yellow glow and transfer it immediately to your vise. Fold the hot steel between the vise-jaws (as described in Chapter 12 on making woodcarving gouges).

Taper the tang and burn it into the wooden handle. If the handle has a reinforcement ferrule and a slightly smaller predrilled hole, the tang can probably be driven in cold without splitting the handle.

A small *garden hand hoe* can be cut out of a scrap plow disc. Heat the blank and fold it "hot" over the edge of the anvil. Then, while the tool's cutting edge is still dark red hot, quench $1/4$ inch of it in water. That part of it is now hardened, while the unsubmerged portion, which will not suffer strain in use, remains soft.

The little *hand rake* is identical to the hand hoe except for its teeth, which should first be slotted on the abrasive cutoff wheel, then bent hot over the anvil. Harden the teeth tips in the same way as the hoe edge.

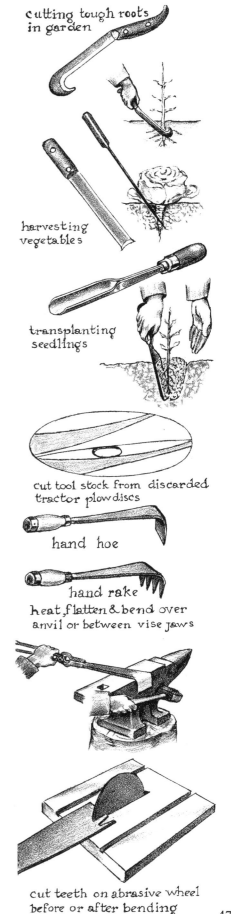

cutting tough roots in garden

harvesting vegetables

transplanting seedlings

cut tool stock from discarded tractor plow discs

hand hoe

hand rake
heat, flatten & bend over anvil or between vise jaws

cut teeth on abrasive wheel before or after bending

stock for cleaver

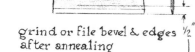

13 2
12
14 4
3 11
1
10

5 6 7 8 9

Salvaged worn steel disc from tractor plow is cut as shown to make stock for tools

heat & flatten on anvil face

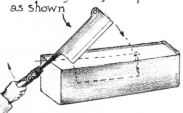

grind or file bevel & edges ½" after annealing

heat in elongated fire ½" to cherry red, and quench as shown

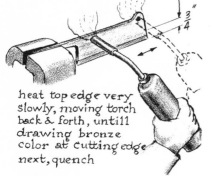

after quenching, polish a sheen for ¾" along edge

3/4"

heat top edge very slowly, moving torch back & forth, until drawing bronze color at cutting edge next, quench

fire clay   fire brick

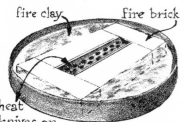

heat knives on long grate blocked in by fire brick & clay placed over forge-grate

48

KITCHEN CLEAVER

Often called a butcher's cleaver, this axlike instrument is invaluable in cutting up meat, bones, and frozen foods of all sorts.

Discarded plow discs are useful, both in their shape and high-carbon quality, as stock for cleavers. (These plow discs come in various sizes and are good to have on hand in your scrap pile for other tools, as well.)

Scribe the blade design you have in mind on the disc. Cut out the blank on your abrasive cutoff wheel, or use a welder's torch. In this event, grind off every trace of steel residue left by the melting action of the welder's torch. You will now have a "clean" disc section, whose thinner outer edge will form the cleaver's blade, and whose thicker center portion becomes the cleaver's spine and tang.

Heat the blank in the forge fire, and hammer out the disc's curve on the anvil. Let it cool slowly, then file, drill, or grind this annealed blank into its final shape.

Now heat the blade, in an elongated fire, as shown. Temper the cleaver just like a broad-blade wood chisel (see Chapter 8) but use a long quenching trough and a propane torch for local annealing. Either burn the tang into the handle, as described in Chapter 10, or rivet it between two wood pieces, as with the sloyd knife.

9. Making Eyebolts and Hooks

Eyebolts and hooks are basic devices for fastening one element to another: gate and door latches; anchors for rope or chain, etc.

Use mild-steel stock, which, if ⅜ of an inch in diameter or less, can be cold-bent in the vise. If thicker stock is used, heat it in the forge first (unless you happen to own a very sturdy vise of fifty pounds or better).

To make the eyebolt, hammer 3 inches of a ⅜-inch rod over the anvil horn until it bends into a 1-inch curve, as shown.

Now seat a 1-inch-diameter steel bar in the curve of the bent rod and clamp the two firmly in the vise. The bolt is formed by hammering first the upright shank end 45° off the vertical. Next, close the eye end by hammering it down flush with the forming bar.

Then remove the whole assembly (forming bar included) from the vise and place the eye over the anvil edge. Hammer out any misalignment, then knock out the forming bar and clamp the eye in the vise. Use a ⅜-inch threading die to thread about 1½ inches of the eyebolt shank-end.

The hook starts out as an eyebolt, but instead of threading the shank, bend it into a hook, just as you did when forming the eye — only leave the end open, as shown.

To link the eyes of hook and bolt, spread one of the eyes open, hook it into the closed eye, then clamp it closed again, either with a hammer or the vise.

A standard latching assembly requires two eyebolts and one hook. The eyebolt through which the hook falls may have to be slightly longer than the eyebolt to which the hook is linked.

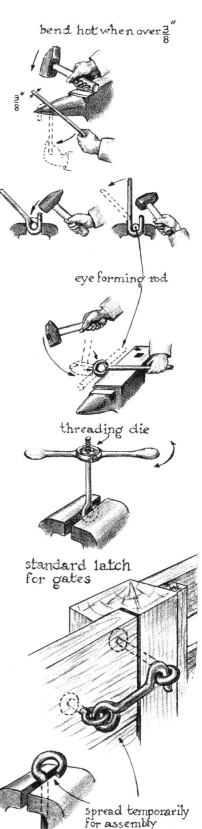

bend hot when over ⅜"

⅜"

eye forming rod

threading die

standard latch for gates

spread temporarily for assembly

10. Making Tool Handles

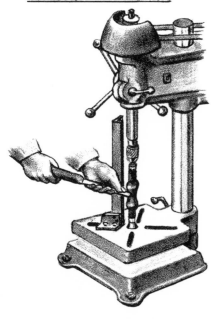

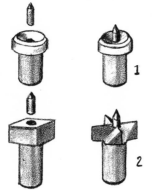

A standard wood lathe is always horizontal, and more convenient, but not having one perhaps you can adjust yourself easily to a "vertical" lathe to cut the wood for your handles. The drill press can be converted into such a vertical lathe on which to turn wooden tool handles. Once you get used to this vertical, instead of horizontal, lathe-turning, you will find it satisfactory. (For lathe tools, follow the method described in Chapter 7.)

CONVERTING THE DRILL PRESS INTO A LATHE

The first step in making a vertical wood lathe is to improvise a tool rest to guide your lathe tool. Rivet together a section of heavy-gauge angle iron and a piece of ¼- to ⅜-inch-thick angle iron, as shown. Then drill a ½-inch hole at the base angle iron to receive the bolt that anchors this tool rest on the drill base.

To make the lathe centers, two ½-inch cap screws (or tap bolts) are used. With a $^3/_{16}$-inch drill, center a ½-inch-deep hole in the head of each cap screw. These holes will later receive snug-fitting pointed pins, which impale the wooden handle stock at either end for stable lathe-turning. You can make these pins by cutting off the pointed ends of two $^3/_{16}$-inch-diameter nails.

File the butterfly headstock, as shown, and tamp in its ½-inch center pin. Then clamp this assembly in the drill-press chuck.

Now countersink the tailstock, using a ½-inch drill; then, either with a file or power grinder, grind the square head round until it forms a knifelike edge with the countersunk depression. Tamp in the second ½-inch center pin and seat this assembly in the base of the drill press. Your converted wood lathe is now prepared to turn whatever handle stock you choose.

It is perhaps worth noting that, for this very operation — grinding the corners off a square-headed cap screw — this vertical lathe would come in handy, since at the drill press's lowest speed, even steel can be ground successfully. You simply brace a file between vertical tool rest and rotating cap screw; this "filing" action quickly and accurately rounds off the screw head — or any other piece of metal that must be turned, provided the part has first been previously ground by hand the approximate diameter needed. Once I realized how well this works, I acquired a carbide-tipped tool for just such improvised metal-turning by hand.

STOCK FOR TOOL HANDLES

Now that your converted wood lathe is ready, it is time to select handle stock to turn in it. Hard, fibrous wood, such as black or English walnut, eucalyptus, ash, hickory, acacia, maple, and comparable woods stand up very well. The wood fibers should always be *straight,* in order to transfer the force of the hammer blows effectively. When the butt end of a wood handle has been plied by hammer extensively, it should begin to fray, like the end of a rope; if, instead, the butt end pulverizes, that type of wood should be avoided in the future. Never use burled wood for handle stock; such wood is "rubbery" and tends to disperse force and thus waste it.

SHAPING THE HANDLE

First, cut the stock to the desired length and thickness. Then drill, in each end, a centered $^3/_{16}$-inch-diameter hole to a depth of ¼ inch.

The end that is to be anchored by the butterfly headstock should have a ⅛-inch-deep X cut in it in which to set the four wing edges. This is made with a saw bisecting the leading hole at right angles.

Adjust your drill head and tool rest to accommodate the handle blank. Rub candle wax on the bottom of the blank to lubricate it, then center it on the drill press. Next, set drill speed at about 2000 rpm (somewhat faster than the standard 1750 rpm electric motor speed). Place wood between centers. Before switching on the motor, carefully align butterfly headstock with the prepared center hole and saw slots in the wood blank. Press the tail end firmly onto the tail center. Release the pressure slightly, and switch on the motor.

Once the wood is spinning, gently lower the drill-press head enough so it countersinks the wood on the tail center; then lock the drill head at that position.

You are now ready to turn a wood handle, using the lathe tools as shown in the standard horizontal wood-lathe setup. Whether you use the latter, or the vertical drill-press conversion, the principles of wood-lathe-turning apply equally and the steps are the same.

The proper angle, or stance, of wood-lathe tool to handle stock is one you must gauge for yourself; only experience, after your first tries, can tell you which tool position works best for you. Obviously, the sharper the tool edge, the smoother the wood surface becomes. However, a major rule of thumb is to keep the gap between tool rest and spinning wood to a minimum. And, whether the tool rest is horizontal or vertical, press the lathe tool down onto the tool rest firmly and hold it steadily as you move your hands along the tool rest.

The shape of a tool handle is a matter of personal preference, and can vary in length, slenderness, or stubbiness, depending on the tool's size and intended use. The handle shown here (some 5 to 6 inches long) has proved to be both practical and all-purpose. But once you have chosen a design and turned the handle accordingly, you are ready to tackle the other tool parts.

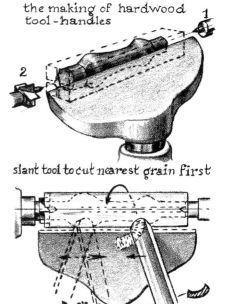

the making of hardwood tool-handles

slant tool to cut nearest grain first

horizontal standard wood lathe setup

FERRULES

Ferrules are metal reinforcement collars, banded around the ends of wooden handles to keep them from splitting. Ferrules can be made from electric conduit pipe of various diameters, as well as metal tubing of many kinds — rifle cartridges, CO_2 cartridges, lipstick tubes. All make effective ferrules when cut into sections.

Use a hacksaw, a pipe cutter, or your abrasive cutoff wheel to cut the length appropriate for each tool. Remove any burrs caused by this cutting with a file or grinding wheel. A rotary file mounted in the drill chuck and run at medium speed is ideal — both for removing burrs and for beveling the inside of ferrules. (An old round hand file, broken into several pieces, makes a fine rotary file. Saw shops often discard ones that you can probably use for this purpose.)

Use one square-holed washer between tool shoulder and the handle. Since tangs are best when square in cross-section (to keep them from loosening and turning in the handle), the washers must fit the square at the point where the tool's shoulder meets it. The main purpose of the washer is to prevent a small shoulder from entering the wood handle under forceful hammer blows when the tool is in use. If the tool's shoulder should be large, a washer is not needed. There are three possible methods of "squaring" a round-holed washer, any one of which will work:

(1) Choose a standard steel bolt washer whose hole is a size smaller than the tool's tang. Clamp the washer lip in your vise so that the hole is free and clear. Use a small square file to square the hole to fit the tang.

(2) Instead of a file, you can use a narrow cold chisel (same width as the tang), shearing the steel flush along the vise jaw, as shown.

(3) A third method is to clamp the tool shank tightly in the vise and slip the undersized washer over the upright tang (it will get hung up about halfway down). Then, take a 5-inch section of ⅜- to ½-inch plumbing pipe and drop it down on the tang so that it sits on the washer. Grease the tang (the part exposed below) a little, and hammer the pipe down until the washer has been forced flush with the tool shoulder. The mild-steel washer yields to the harder steel of the tang. This partly cuts the washer steel and partly compresses it, forcing it tightly onto the shoulder ledges.

It is often difficult to true up shoulder ledges accurately. A simple method is to clamp the tool shoulder (tang upright) in your vise, leaving about ⅛ of an inch of shoulder protruding above the jaws. Slip a fairly large washer (thinner than ⅛ of an inch, but larger than the tool shoulder) over tang and shoulder so that it rests loosely on the vise jaws. With a flat file, cut away any shoulder "excess" around the tang, using the washer as a trueing jig. The washer also acts as a tool rest, keeping the file clear of the vise so that neither it nor the file can be harmed. To remain strong, the tang must be thickest at its shoulder location. Make sure, therefore, that the file's edge does not groove the tang accidentally while you are filing the shoulder flush with the washer.

square-holed washer

tube forces washer onto tool shoulder

washer is jig to help file shoulder accurately

file shoulder

FITTING HANDLES TO FERRULES

Each ferrule should have one inside-bevel end. The bevel, when pressed over a slightly oversized handle end, will not cut the wood but squeeze it in a tight fit with the ferrule. You can measure the precise fit by pressing the sharp edge of the ferrule onto a slightly tapered handle end. This pressure leaves a circular dent on the wood, indicating how much you still need to cut off, yet leaving enough so that the beveled ferrule end will squeeze onto the handle under great pressure when it is hammered, or pressed on, as shown.

One more step may be needed. If the wood chosen for the handle was not adequately seasoned (dried out), shrinkage would eventually loosen the end ferrule. To prevent that, hammer a few depressions in the ferrule (once it's seated) with a center punch. This locks the ferrule to the wood with little dowel-like points. Subsequent hammering, while using the tool, will eventually expand the wood enough to "fill" the ferrule, and thus anchor it permanently.

FINISHING THE HANDLE

Once the ferrules are pressed and locked on, center the assembled handle once again in the lathe and trim off any excess wood.

At this point, either dismount the improvised vertical tool rest (if you are using the converted drill press) or move the standard horizontal tool rest well away from the handle. This clears the work area for the hand sanding and polishing which you now begin.

Refine the handle with progressively finer abrasive paper, until it is extremely smooth. Then, with the handle still spinning, hold a little wad of shellac-soaked cloth against it to seal the wood. Now, before the shellac dries, hold a piece of beeswax against the spinning handle, to act as a lubricant while polishing the surface. The last step is to hold a dry, clean wad of cloth firmly against the spinning handle, moving it back and forth as a final buffing.

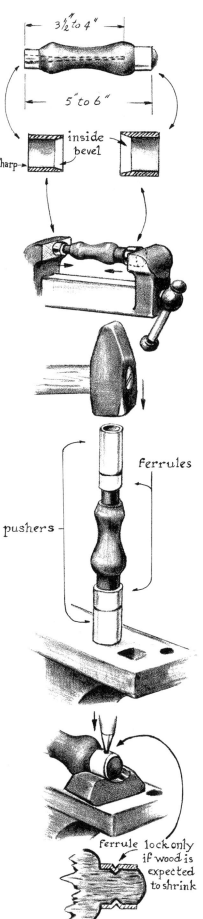

burning tool tang into a wooden handle

heat ¾" tang tip

I

II

III

$\frac{1}{8}$"

IV

heat light cherry red

tempering tool blade after assembly

↓ quench

↓ draw color over gas flame

ASSEMBLING HANDLE AND TOOL

Assuming that your tool blank has already been tempered, and fitted snugly in the square-holed washer, you should now drill a ⅛-inch tang-hole in the 5- to 6-inch handle deep enough to hold a 3½- to 4-inch tool tang. Heat the tang in your forge fire until ¾ of an inch of its tip shows a dark heat glow. This indicates, because of heat conductivity, that the whole tang is hot enough to burn into wood, without risking temper loss to tool shank or blade (should they have been previously tempered).

Clamp the tool shank (tang upward) in the vise and quickly slip the handle down over the hot tang. Let both flame and smoke escape while you rapidly, but lightly, hammer the handle down until it is ⅛ of an inch short of the shoulder washer. Let the whole assembly cool somewhat; then "cinch" the handle down on the tool flush with the washer, thereby seating and holding the burned-in tang permanently. There is now little chance that the handle will split, even with maximum use, since the wood, which became temporarily soft where the hot tang contacted the wood, once again becomes resiliently hard after final cinching and complete cooling.

TEMPERING THE TOOL BLADE

You may find that a tool blade occasionally has to be tempered (or retempered) after it has been burned into its handle. In such an instance, wind a wet strip of cloth around the handle to keep the wood from scorching. Then heat the tool blade to a light cherry glow, quench, and finally, after polishing the blade mirror-smooth, draw the temper color over a blue gas flame.

11. Making Hammers

HAMMER DESIGN

In toolmaking, the hammer is an all-important tool. In order to design one that meets its function perfectly, you must first understand the principle of hammering.

A hammer's prime purpose is to release stored energy, on impact. A hammer that strikes a chisel to cut wood must deliver the right amount of energy to make the cut without overloading the chisel so that it bends or breaks. The size of the chisel, the hardness of the wood, and the weight of the hammer must all be correlated. The craftsman should learn to "feel" the ideal relationship, or harmony, between the three elements. Choosing the right weight of hammer (whether it is made of steel, plastic, wood, or rawhide) for the job at hand can prevent frustration, and save time and energy when work is to continue hour after hour.

This same "feel" applies in choosing *any* tool for a given task, even if you simply want to hammer a nail into wood.

Hammer Weight

If you try to drive a thin nail into hard wood, many light taps with a lightweight hammer works best; a heavy hammer would collapse such a thin nail.

To drive a sturdy nail into hard wood, deliver several well-directed medium blows with a medium-weight hammer; too heavy a hammer might collapse such a nail if the wood is very hard.

To drive a heavy spike into hard wood, a heavy hammer, delivering many well-directed blows, will be needed.

Of course, there is a point when even the sturdiest nail or spike will collapse under heavy blows with a heavy hammer if the wood is too hard. Then, only predrilling a slightly undersized hole to receive the nail or spike will work.

relating hammer weight to size of tool & hardness of wood

relating hammer weight to size of nail, hardness of wood

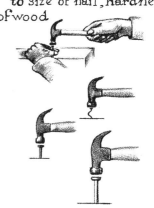

drill when wood is too hard

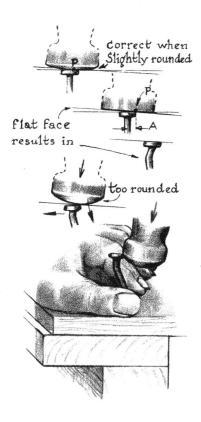

flat face
results in

carpenter's hammer

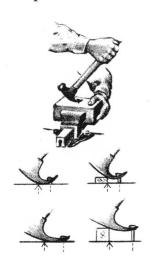

shoemaker's hammer

The Face

Most hand-held hammers that have hard faces have one design feature in common: a slightly rounded face.

The reason becomes clear once you try to use a flat-faced hammer on a standard flat-headed nail. As shown, a slightly unaligned blow (on a slant, instead of parallel to the face of the nailhead) contacts the nailhead at point P; the force of the blow, delivered from distance A toward the center of the nail stem, will either bend the nail, as shown, or cause the hammer to glance off.

This same unaligned blow, delivered by a slightly rounded hammer face, contacts the nail head at P so close to the center of the nail stem that it will not bend.

But, note that too rounded a face spells trouble — in the form of a bloody thumb and finger!

Since hand-hammering is necessarily less precise than machine-hammering, this slightly rounded hammer face design allows the craftsmen a margin of human error, but near-machine precision.

The Claw

When nails are not driven accurately — or permanently — they must be extracted. Thus, a *claw* was added to the hammer's design, giving us the present-day carpenter's hammer.

The curve of the claw varies to meet the needs of pulling out different nails. A steeply curved claw works best to pull out a large nail that is firmly held in the wood; but it is slow work and requires the aid of progressively bigger props. A flatter claw will pull out a small nail that is not held too firmly in a couple of tugs, with or without a prop.

The Stem

The length of the hammer stem (handle) depends on the craftman's needs. For example, a long stem can be a great impediment when you are doing close work hour after hour, in cramped quarters. Conversely, if a great deal of heavy hammering must be done — large spikes, hard wood — a short stem would soon exhaust you. Generally speaking, stem length is determined by hammer head weight, which in turn is determined by the magnitude of the task at hand. A tack hammer is short-stemmed and lightweight; a sledgehammer is long-stemmed and heavyweight.

A shoemaker's hammer is specifically designed so that the cobbler can drive in short-stemmed tacks with broad flat heads, without denting the surrounding leather. Such a hammer has a large, flat face, a slightly rounded rim, and is fairly light in weight. In one stroke, the tack automatically aligns itself with the hammer face. Such tack hammers are also used by carpet-layers and upholsterers, who have to tack carpeting or material tight without crushing fiber or fabric. These hammers often have magnetized faces, to which tacks "stick." The upholsterer thus has both hands free, one to wield the hammer and the other to stretch the material tight. In short, analyzing your needs correctly will lead to logical design of the hammers you make.

THE CROSS PEEN HAMMER

Shown here is a simple, all-purpose, lightweight hammer with a double-duty head: one end has a slightly rounded face; the other, a cross peen. It is useful in many shop activities — driving nails and forming heads on small rivets, bending light-gauge metal parts in the vise, etc.

Begin with a rod of high-carbon steel that is ¾ to 1 inch in diameter. (You can use a square cross-section bar, a torsion bar, or a car axle, should your scrap pile yield these.)

Clamp the end of the rod into the drill vise and make two center-punch marks ⅜ of an inch apart; then drill two holes, ⅜ of an inch in diameter, through the bar at these marks. If the steel is too hard to drill, heat it in the forge and cool it slowly in ashes to anneal it.

The holes, made by a ⅜-inch drill, should be close together but just missing one another. Be sure that they are exactly centered (not lopsided) in the bar.

Now select a ⅜-inch-diameter mild-steel rod and saw off two sections 1-inch long to be used as plugs. Dent them with a few hammer blows on the anvil so that they will "grab" when pounded into the two prepared holes. Once the plugs are in place, grind off any excess so their heads are flush with the rod surface.

Drill a third hole, midway between the first two, then drive out the two plug remnants. You will end up with a roughly oval hole, as shown. Smooth out the inside with a hand file.

Now fashion the cross peen, either by grinding it on a motor grinder, or cutting it with a hacksaw. Cut off the last 3 inches of the rod with a hacksaw to form the hammer head.

blacksmith's hammer

1" DIA.

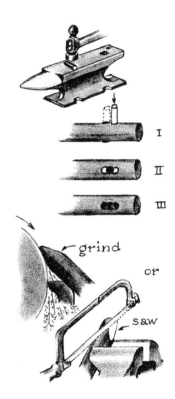

I

II

III

grind

or

saw

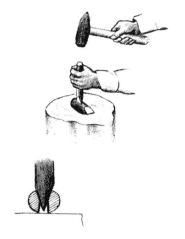

Place this blank on your freestanding wood stump and insert a ¾-inch cold chisel into the oval hole, as a wedge. Holding the chisel firmly in vise-grip pliers or tongs, use your heaviest bench hammer to drive the chisel in until it spreads the sides of the steel blank slightly. This gives you a roughly conical hole, into which the wooden stem will later be locked. Knock out the cold chisel (easy, because of its taper) and your hammer blank is now ready for tempering.

String a piece of baling wire through the hammer hole so that you can submerge the whole blank in the forge fire, as shown. When it glows a dark cherry red, quench it at once deep in oil, moving the hammer head up and down a little to speed the cooling somewhat.

Any piece of hot steel as large as this blank will require at least five gallons of oil for adequate quenching. Old crankcase oil will work very well, but make sure your oil container has a hinged lid so that you can close it quickly to snuff out accidental flash fires.

Since the hammer head has become thin on both sides of the hole, quenching in water is too risky; the steel may well crack at such vulnerable points.

Test the cooled steel for hardness with the file tip, pressing down firmly. (Never apply full file strokes on hardened steel for you will ruin your file in short order.) Recall that if the file tip slides off like a needle on glass, your steel is sufficiently hard.

Now anneal the sides of the hole to prevent the hammer head from breaking there during severe use.

This local annealing can be accomplished while simultaneously tempering the hammer head as a whole. Grind the sides of the hammer on the rubber-backed sanding disc until a mirror-smooth sheen appears from end to end.

Now take a ¾-inch-diameter mild-steel rod and grind its end flat and tapered, like a cold chisel, so that it will slip loosely into the hammer hole.

Heat the tapered rod end in the fire. When it becomes yellow hot, hold it upright and slip the hardened hammer blank on it. Hold it above the water bucket and watch for a yellow oxidation color to spread to both ends of the blank. At this point, the sides of the hole will be purple, whereupon you should immediately knock the blank off the rod and into the water bucket.

Once it is quenched and cool, hold the blank at right angles to your rubber-backed abrasive disc to true up the hammer face (check with your square for accuracy, as shown).

As you proceed to grind, rotating the blank over the spinning disc, you will find that the natural limitations of hand work result in concentric inaccuracies. Instead of a perfectly flat surface, the hammer face will become just slightly rounded — but symmetrically so, and therefore exactly what you need!

Now prepare a 10- to 12-inch hammer stem made of ash, hickory, eucalyptus, or any hard-fiber wood of your choice. Drive it into the smaller opening of the conical oval hole.

Make a steel wedge out of a thick nail by cold-hammering its end into a taper on the anvil. Score it with a cold chisel to make sure it holds tightly when driven into the wood. Drive the nail wedge in diagonally, as far as it will go, thereby spreading the wooden stem to fill the cone-shaped hole. Cut the nail excess off with a hacksaw and grind it flush with the hammer head.

Check to make sure that the stem is correctly aligned with the hammer head, from all angles. If stem alignment is off, but the wood is thick enough, reshape it with a wood rasp or sanding disc, as shown. If the stem is askew (as shown in profile), nothing can be done but to cut it off where it enters the hammer and punch out the wasted piece. You will lose that length when refitting the stem, but enough may remain to be refitted accurately.

You have now completed a well-tempered, all-purpose hammer for your collection, and, at the same time, learned the principles to apply in making future hammers of different design.

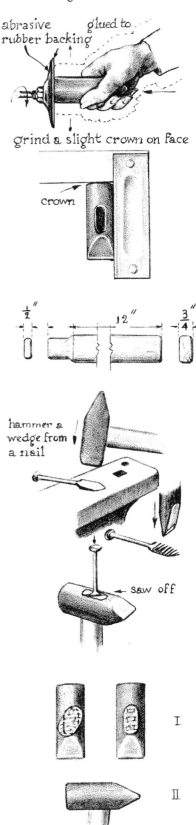

making a hammer

abrasive rubber backing glued to

grind a slight crown on face

crown

hammer a wedge from a nail

saw off

I

II

12. Making Sculptors' Woodcarving Gouges

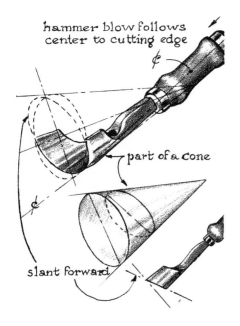

hammer blow follows center to cutting edge

part of a cone

slant forward

Follows curves without binding

because blade is part of a cone

DESIGN OF THE SCULPTORS' WOODCARVING GOUGE

This chapter is concerned mainly with sculptors' woodcarving gouges, yet the design principles are basic to almost any wood gouge or chisel.

Other crafts may require particular features in woodcarving tools that are not present in sculptors' gouges. For instance, certain crafts use chisels to *pry* with (as in making mortise-joint seats); to *scrape-cut* (deep wooden bowls); or to *plane* (a millwright's slick).

The function of the sculptor's woodcarving gouge is simply to remove chips of wood, much as a beaver does when felling a tree. The tool design, as shown, becomes self-explanatory. If a chisel has the conventional "cylindrical" type blade, it cannot help but bind as it cuts a deep groove, especially in a curve. Note, then, the difference of the "cone" type blade, and how, without resisting sideways guidance, the cone design allows the blade to follow the carver's manipulation.

The illustration shows how the cutting edge should be tailored so that the *upper* part of the edge slants forward. This blade design ensures that the outer grain (fiber) of the wood is cut first, thus freeing and releasing the woodchip without binding.

Conventional chisels have the lower part of their cutting edge ground to protrude forward. This results in a "wedge" action, in which chips can be released only after forced driving. That same force will often tear the outer fibers, instead of cutting them, especially in a hard or brittle wood. Soft wood can be cut well enough if the conventional chisel is thin, since the wedge action of the tool hardly compacts the wood. But the hard mallet or hammer blows required to free chips tend to bend or break such a thin tool, making it a liability at best.

All woodcarving gouges that are hand-held can profit from the conical design. When modified by the inventive craftsman, they can serve the most unexpected woodcarving needs (bowl- and scroll-carving, cutting letters in signboards, marking measuring scales, for instance).

It may interest the reader to know that this cone blade design, though probably not "new" in a historical sense, came to me many years ago when I began to design woodcarving tools for my own use. I had found that commercial chisels were not adequate for wood sculpture, and so began to design my own. The cone blade quickly caught on with other sculptors, who saw it as the ideal answer to their particular needs.

basic design principle for woodcarving gouges

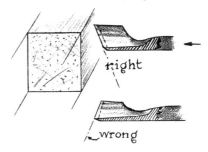

right

wrong

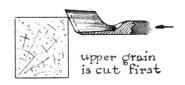

upper grain is cut first

therefore all lower grain is cut next, freeing chip to come loose easily

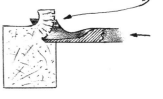

SMALL WOODCARVING GOUGES

The hand-pushed engraver's-style small woodcarving gouge, as shown, is adapted from the wood-engraver's burin. Thus, the woodcarver can utilize the engraver's flexible hand and tool manipulation when he works with a small gouge.

The most distinctive feature of the engraver's-style gouge is its flat upright shank, traditionally designed so that the thumb, braced firmly against it, acts as an anchor as well as a guide along which the tool slides as it cuts. The tool is held by the fingers, while the handle is cushioned against the heel of the hand and is pushed by contraction of the hand muscles. For increased stability and reduced danger of the tool shooting forward, which so often happens in conventional handling of carving tools, the thumb is securely anchored down on the wood by the other thumb (see photographs, pages 86–7). Applying the traditional wood-engraving tool design and manipulation to small sculpture carving gouges gives magnificent control as well as flexibility in straightforward or curved-form wood cutting. In addition, the flat upright shank sliding against the thumb cannot cut into it, whereas the standard commercial tool, with its small sharp-edged square shank, can.

hand pushed engraver style small woodcarving gouges

4½" to 5"

Wood-engraving burins, small sculptors' wood gouges, as well as wood-block and linoleum-block gouges, can all be made without the advanced skills of the blacksmith, though you will need a forge for minor shaping and, of course, for tempering.

A 1/8-inch-deep Gouge

Cut a 6-inch length of a ¼- to ⁵/₁₆-inch-diameter high-carbon steel rod. Spring steel from a straightened coil spring is excellent for this purpose.

Place this annealed rod upright in your drill vise and, with a ⅛-inch drill, center a hole ¾ of an inch deep. Be sure that you drill in the exact center of the rod. An eccentric hole is dangerous because the drill may accidentally break when it comes through a thin part, and become lodged there.

Keep small drills razor-sharp and symmetrically ground to avoid wandering action that causes such strains and breaks. Progress a little at a time, withdrawing the drill often to remove steel pulp. Use lard as a cutting agent.

Next, grind or file the tool blank, as shown. Refine its texture using rubber-backed abrasive discs, and grind an outside bevel to form the tool's cutting edge. Finally, temper the tool blade.

If all has gone well, the drill track should have a smooth final and finished texture, and the blank is now ready to be joined to a handle.

Note that from now on the razor-sharp and hard-tempered cutting edge of the gouge is a present danger at each step during the assembly of tool and handle. Therefore, *be careful* of the gouge when it is clamped in the vise for further work, and *never* leave its blade exposed when you are away from it, even temporarily. You, or someone else in the shop, could be severely injured by bumping into that lethal edge.

Somewhat wider deep gouges are made in the same way.

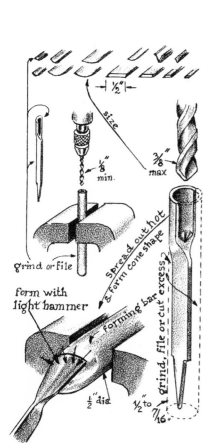

grind or file

form with
light hammer

size

½"

⅛" min.

⅜" max

spread out hot
& form cone shape

forming bar

grind, file or cut excess

½" dia

½ to ⁷/₁₆"

A Wide-Bladed Engraver's-Style Gouge

When finished, this gouge will have a 1-inch-radius blade curve. Begin as you did in making the small gouge. Select a ¾-inch-diameter high-carbon steel rod and drill it with a ⅜-inch drill. File or grind off the excess to arrive at the blank's blade, as shown by dotted lines.

Clamp a ½-inch-diameter forming bar in your vise to act as a "saddle." Excellent "saddles" can be filed or ground from car bumpers, and plumbing pipes and fittings; halves of pulleys and ball-bearing races. These can be filed or ground into smooth-surfaced forming bars or saddles. Shaping saddles can be devised from most any concave or convex steel implement, provided it is sufficiently resistant and of the proper diameter. Plumbing pipes (as shown), old pillow blocks, halves of steel collars, pulleys, and gear hubs — all make good forming saddles with varying diameters, giving you plenty of choice for whatever gouge curves you want to make.

It is best to preheat the saddle a little with a propane torch before placing the gouge blade on it. This way the thin hot blade does not cool so fast and stays malleable longer, and the work in reshaping it may be done in one heating period, after some experience. (If the saddle is icy cold, a thin hot blade placed on it will be "hardened" as if quenched. Preheating the saddle to about 300° C. (572° F.) is a good habit.)

Heat the tool blade in the forge to a yellow glow and place it over the preheated saddle. Using a ½- to ¾-pound hammer, tap quickly but lightly on the blade blank, starting with the thicker curved portion (where the material resists reshaping most) and working progressively outward toward the thinner end (cutting edge) of the blade. Rapid, even, and gentle strokes over the whole surface will shape the blade accurately over the saddle curve. Reheat the blade periodically if it becomes too cool.

Try to keep the tool's shank and blade well aligned while hammering; if the blank "twists," make sure it is hot, then wrench it back with tongs or pliers.

Complete the blank as with the other small gouges.

Finishing Gouges

Unlike the engraver's-style and V-shaped gouges we have discussed, small finishing gouges are sometimes so shallow they are almost flat; thus, they can be made from flat steel stock. A broken starter spring, a heavy-gauge clock spring, or a section of a handsaw are all good stock.

Heat the shank section of the stock to a yellow glow and clamp its lower part in the vise. Then, with tongs, twist the exposed upright portion 90°, as shown. Align the shank and blade on the anvil face with a hammer.

This shaping method applies to all *flat* small gouges; the desired width of blade can be ground or filed later on, at the time you fashion the tang. Making these flat gouge blanks can be the first steps in making deeper curved roughing out gouges as well as shallow curved finishing gouges.

Once gouge blanks have been shaped, aligned, filed, ground, and polished, they are finished by tempering and sharpening. Finally the tangs can be burned into wooden handles as described on page 64.

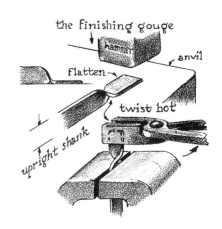

the finishing gouge
hammer
anvil
flatten
twist hot
upright shank

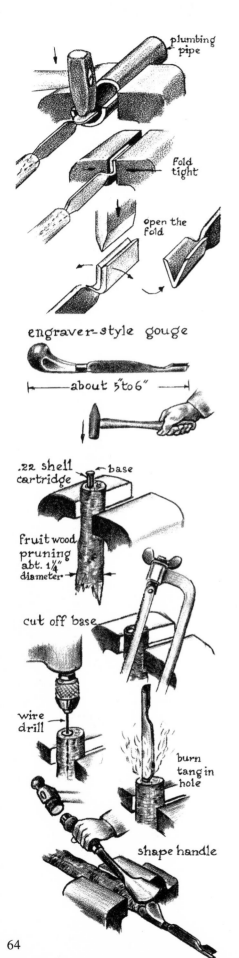

plumbing pipe

Fold tight

open the fold

engraver-style gouge

|— about 5″to 6″ —|

.22 shell cartridge ← base

fruit wood pruning abt. 1¼″ diameter·

cut off base

wire drill

burn tang in hole

shape handle

A V-shaped Gouge Made by Folding

If a flat blade is hammered on to a curved saddle, as shown, it can be reheated and folded in the vise as the first step in making a V gouge.

To open the hot folded blade, use a flat cold chisel with double-beveled edge as a wedge, as shown. If no one is available to help you hold the blank on the flat anvil face, you can put the cold chisel in the vise (cutting edge up). Hold the heated blank with tongs, and place the folded blade on the chisel. Hammer the blade open with a flat wooden stick (so as not to dent the outside of the V-shaped blade).

Reheat the blank once more, and again place it over the cold chisel in the vise. Now refine the blade alignment and the final angle of the V.

With practice, you can use this method for making V-shaped tools with very small angles. By filing down the excess of the blade uprights, the tool will become fine enough to cut lines of hairline widths on wood blocks.

An important feature here is that the strains involved in cutting minute lines are so small that you can afford an almost ''brittle'' hardness in tempering the very end of the blade, and if not abused, such tools never need to be resharpened.

Small-Tool Handles

Fruitwood makes excellent handles for small tools, but the wood need not be too hard. From your garden, or orchard (or even a friend's firewood supply), select straight, dead branches about 1 to 1¼ inches thick and at least 10 inches long. Fruitwood prunings salvaged from local orchards are a fine source of supply.

Preferably, the handle should have a small ferrule reinforcing it where it joins the tang (see pages 52–3, on ferrules). Suitable stock for such ferrules includes small brass tubing, or empty .22 pistol or rifle cartridges.

Clamp the branch vertically in the vise and lightly tap (with a ¼-pound hammer) the .22 cartridge into the branch, as shown, leaving $1/16$ of an inch of its base exposed. Cut off this base with a hacksaw so that the ferrule is flush with the wood.

Taper-file a $1/16$-inch-diameter nail stem to make a wire drill. Then drill this wire down into the branch, in the dead center of the .22 cartridge. The improvised mild-steel drill will get hot and burn itself in, preparing a hole for the gouge tang.

Heat the tool tang somewhat, then gently drive it straight into the hole with a wooden mallet until it seems secure.

If you prefer, reverse the procedure by clamping the tool shank in the vise, hot tang upright. Then slip the prepared branch over the hot tang and tap it down as far as you think necessary. Whichever method you choose, keep both tool and branch aligned throughout.

Now, with the tool well secured, reclamp the branch horizontally in the vise, allowing a 2½- to 3-inch overhang, as shown.

Use a flat carpenter's chisel (or a larger wood gouge, if you've made one) with a half-pound mallet or hammer, to carve the branch as shown. Once the handle has been shaped, use a hacksaw or coping saw to incise the branch where it meets the handle to ⅜ of an inch all around. Use a 1-inch cone-blade gouge, as shown, to round off the handle; when only a core of wood remains, cut the handle off with a hacksaw. Now refine the whole handle, with rasp, abrasive paper, or on your rubber-backed abrasive wheel.

The experience gained in making the small woodcarving gouge should enable you now to make a whole set of small gouges, as simple or elaborate as your talent allows and your needs dictate. They will prove ideal for the carving of small sculptures, low-relief work, cameos, linoleum blocks, side-grain wood blocks, and many other jobs requiring only small tools.

A Small V-shaped Gouge

The V-shaped cutting edge of a veining tool will prove more difficult to make than the previous gouge design. The very bottom of the V seems to resist most efforts to create a truly sharp meeting place of the two upright sides of the tool. I believe the most direct way to make this tool by hand is to use a triangular file and a steel cutting chisel ground to the same angle as the file.

Stock for this gouge can be a straightened ⅜-inch-diameter coil spring. Heat it in the forge and bend 1 inch of the hot end to a 45° angle, as shown. Then let the hot metal anneal by placing it in ashes for twenty minutes. If still too hot to handle, quench the blank in water and clamp it firmly in the vise. Use the small triangular file and in the bent section file a groove as even as your skill allows. Reheat in fire to yellow glow; then straighten, align, and anneal.

The natural limitation in sharpness of any file will prevent you from making the bottom of the groove really sharp. Thus it is time to turn to a triangular cold-chisel-type tool.

Grind the chisel to the identical angle of the triangular file, but sharpen only its very bottom cutting edge, as shown. Leave the chisel's upright edges dull but polished: this ensures a perfect alignment of chisel in groove, and protects the gouge's filed uprights against scoring by chisel and hammer action.

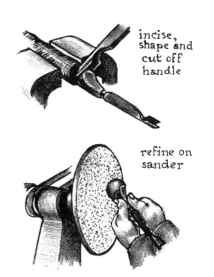

incise, shape and cut off handle

refine on sander

making a small V gouge

bend hot a ⅜ dia. high-carbon steel rod

file groove

straighten while hot

rounded groove sharpened

grind to fit groove as shown

sharp polished & dull

65

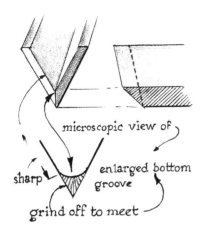

microscopic view of

sharp

enlarged bottom groove

grind off to meet

finished tool

made from high-carbon thin L

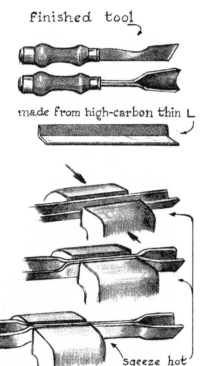

squeeze hot

bend — hammer out & form hot

anvil horn

Align the chisel in the tool's groove, and cut as sharp a groove as possible, with many light hammer taps (instead of a few hard blows) to cut the very bottom of the groove sharp.

LARGE WOODCARVING GOUGES

The design features of large woodcarving gouges are the same as for small gouges which are not struck with a mallet or hammer.

High-carbon angle-iron bars salvaged from steel bed frames, garden swings, or dishwashers all make good tool material for large gouges because these articles as a rule are light in weight but very strong. Equally suitable stock for large gouges is the lightweight, yet rigid, steel tubing often used in high-grade bicycle frames.

To make your first large gouge, select an angle bar from a bed frame. Cut off a 20-inch length — long enough to hold by hand during heating in the forge. Heat a 7-inch section (for the shank) to a yellow heat glow in a slightly elongated fire. The heat should be spread as evenly as possible and 1½ inches longer than the vise jaws in which the piece will be clamped later on. Have everything ready so that not a second is wasted when the bar has become hot. Immediately transfer the hot bar to your vise, and tighten the jaws quickly to squeeze the angle sides together until they meet. Repeat this same process for the tang end.

It will take several reheatings to accomplish this forming, but aim for as few as possible since excessive reheating will damage the steel's composition. *Never overheat steel to white hot* (sparks will fly from the fire at such heat), for this is close to the melting point of steel and may ruin it for good.

Now heat the 1½-inch blade end to a yellow heat glow. Place it over the anvil horn, as shown, and flatten out the angle bend with hammer blows, leaving the middle section of the curved blade as thick as possible.

The next heating must be spread evenly over the entire, now slightly curved, blade. Place the hot blade over the anvil horn again, and, with a 1- to 2-pound hammer, tap rapidly down each side, alternately, to bend the blade edges into a gradual curve from shank to blade edge while following the cone shape of the horn as well. This gradual curve between shank and blade allows the hammer blows during woodcarving to be transferred more evenly over the gouge's cutting edge. An abrupt meeting of blade with shank tends to cause breakage where the blade meets the shank, particularly if the tool is somewhat thin at that point.

The final shaping of the blade on the anvil horn should be done with a light hammer. Keep the blade malleable (yellow hot) and in constant alignment with shank and horn as you tap it, now here, now there, in very rapid progression.

Remember, if your first attempt at this shaping of a tool blank is something of a struggle, each time you make another you will benefit from the previous experience. Practice will steadily improve your results.

What you have actually been doing here is what in coppersmithing and sheet metal work is the main skill and activity: it is bending already flattened steel, much as a tailor works with paper. The blacksmith may engage in this type of activity on occasion, but the specialty of his craft is in hammering one given solid volume of hot steel into another shape of the same volume. This *forming* includes "upsetting" (making long pieces of steel shorter) and "drawing-out" (making short pieces longer). Forming steel this way is true forging, whereas *bending* steel may be done without true forging (blacksmith) skill. (Some modern thin mild-steel plates can often be bent and stretched cold, as is done in the automobile industry when whole car body parts are shaped cold in giant dies. No true forging enters into this.)

Your hot-bent work should now have produced a suitable large-gouge blank, as shown. If there is a slight jog between shank and blade, it can be eliminated, though it concerns more the appearance than the effectiveness of the finished gouge. If you wish to bring the bottom of the blade into alignment with the shank, reheat the shank at the jog location and lay the whole tool blank on the anvil face. Deliver one or more exact blows with a medium-heavy hammer, as shown. This will bend out the jog and correct the shank alignment. Any localized spots forced out of true alignment by this hammering can be corrected with light taps. Reheat the blank if necessary.

Finally, grind the blank as shown, removing any steel not needed for tool strength. Where shank and tang meet, leave a notch broad enough to "shoulder" the ferrule of the handle.

If you prefer having a washer between shoulder and handle, it must rest on two small shoulder ledges: heat the area yellow hot and hold the blank over the anvil edge, crease down. A few precise heavy blows will force the shank down, creating a bottom shoulder where it binds at the anvil edge, as shown. Any slight distortion this causes in the blank must be corrected now, while the steel is still hot, and only with the flat of the hammer. Grind the blank at the point where the tang begins, to form the upper shoulder ledge.

Next, clamp the blank firmly in your vise (tang up) and slip a heated, undersized washer over the tang. Have ready a tube a size smaller than the washer to use as a pusher. Quickly hammer the washer down until it is flush with the shoulder ledges, thus forcing a snug fit.

Now wedge the tang into a temporary wooden handle, so that you can hold the tool blank comfortably during its final and precise grinding and sharpening (see page 33).

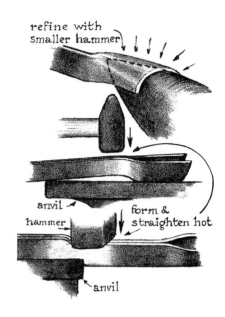

refine with smaller hammer

anvil

hammer

form & straighten hot

anvil

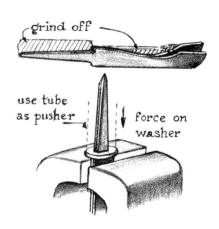

grind off

use tube as pusher

force on washer

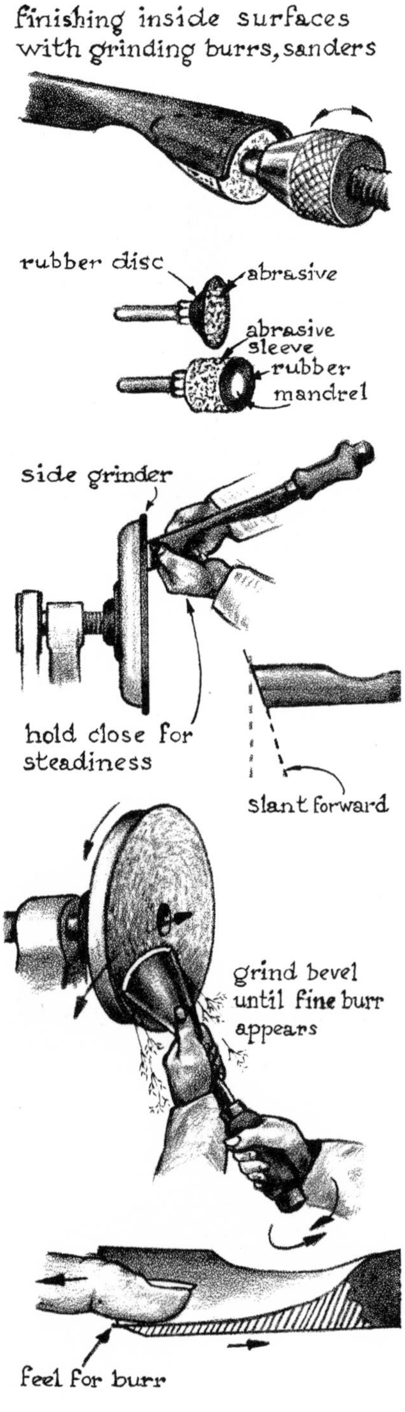

finishing inside surfaces
with grinding burrs, sanders

rubber disc   abrasive

abrasive
sleeve
rubber
mandrel

side grinder

hold close for
steadiness

slant forward

grind bevel
until fine burr
appears

feel for burr

Grinding the Bevel

Refine the inside of the blade with chuck-insert burr grinders and rubber-backed abrasive sleeves of a diameter to match the curve of the blade. Grind the outside of the blade evenly and toward its shoulders, following the conical curves as closely as possible. Then refine the surface with progressively more fine-grit abrasives, finishing up on the buffing wheel to give the blade a mirror sheen.

Begin the grinding of the outside (or cutting edge) bevel by first making a clean, mirror-shiny, cross-sectional cut at the blade-end: take the tool by its blade (both hands as close to the abrasive disc as you dare) and hold it, at a constant angle, to the side-grinder wheel. As soon as the blade-end is ground evenly, scrape off the burr that has formed on its inside with the sharp steel edge of a file tip. You will now see a mirror-shiny cross section, revealing clearly the exact thickness of the blade at the cutting end.

Slanting the tool against the grinding wheel at such an angle that the mirror surface reflects the condition of the edge during grinding, you can guide your movement so as to avoid overgrinding. Only practice will enable you to become skilled at this. The tiniest remaining glimmer of the cross section must gradually disappear, leaving only a faintly noticeable burr. When this burr is felt, as shown, it means that the inside and outside surfaces of the blade's cutting edges have met. (See also the illustration on page 35.) Any further grinding is useless and will only shorten its lifetime.

Removing the Burr

Refine the texture that the grinding has left on the bevel surface with the rubber abrasive wheel, or (in view of what this razor-sharp tool can do to rubber), with an extremely fine-grit abrasive stone wheel.

Next, refine the bevel on your cotton buffing wheel, with tripoli compound rubbed into its spinning buffer face. First, hold the bevel-edge plane tangentially against the rotating wheel rim, so that the cotton fabric slides off the steel as the tool is pressed against it. Then reverse the blade and "grind" the inside of the blade, tangentially. The burr thus is "ground" off (as described in the chapter on tool sharpening).

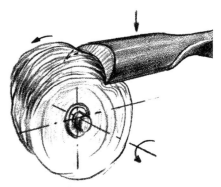

grind off burr on buffer with Tripoli compound

Tempering and Assembly

You may temper the finished tool blank either now, or after its tang has been burned into a permanent handle. In the latter case, the wooden handle should first be wrapped in a wet rag to prevent scorching (see page 54).

When the blade is tempered and blank and handle assembled, test the tool on the wood you plan to carve, allowing the tool its full bite, but never burying the blade so that its whole edge is out of sight. If it does not buckle, crack, or chip, yet scratches the wood surface somewhat, it suggests that a microscopic sawtooth cutting edge still remains. This can be remedied by buffing the bevel a little more on both sides. With that, you will have finished your first large sculptor's gouge and given it an ideally sharp edge.

13. Making a Seating Cutter and Hinge Joints

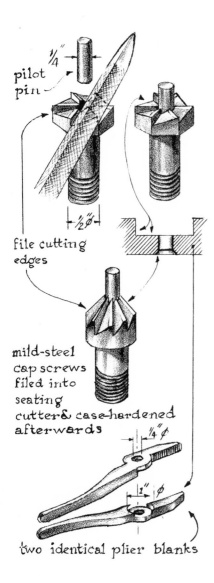

pilot pin

¼"

½"

file cutting edges

mild-steel cap screws filed into seating cutter & case-hardened afterwards

¼" ⌀

1" ⌀

two identical plier blanks

THE SEATING CUTTER

A seating cutter, which sometimes acts as a milling cutter and drill combined, is made here with six cutting teeth and a pilot pin. This ensures precise bearing surfaces for the tools, which, when joined with a hinge pin, achieve the hinging action essential to pliers, shears, tongs, tinsnips, and other hinging tools.

The seating cutter shown here is filed from a standard hexagon-headed ½-inch-diameter mild-steel cap screw, which later is case hardened.

First, drill a $^3/_{16}$-inch pilot-pin hole ¾ of an inch deep into the exact center of the hexagon head. By clamping the cap screw in the drill press vise, you can be sure of drilling the hole dead center, and in true alignment with the cap-screw shank.

File the teeth in the hexagonal pattern, as shown, first with a triangular bastard (medium-coarse) file, then refine with a triangular smooth file.

Lock the cap-screw shank in the drill chuck and place under it, on the drill press table, an abrasive cutoff disc (or salvaged remnant). Set the drill press at medium speed, and lower the cap screw gently onto the abrasive, barely touching it. This action will grind shiny little horizontal facets on the six teeth of the head.

Now clamp the cap screw in the vise, with its teeth up, and with the smooth file sharpen the six cutting edges exactly. All the teeth have the same length so as to mill a perfect plane and absolute circle in your tool blank. Use outside calipers to measure the length of each tooth.

The mild-steel cutter teeth are now ready to be case hardened. A commercial case-hardening compound powder is available in any machinists' supply house. Ask for a non-toxic brand and follow the instructions given on the can.

Build a small, but even and clean, forge fire, and make a little depression with the poker in the fire mound center. Place the cutter blank in it, teeth down. As soon as the end of the blank is medium-yellow hot, lift the cutter out gently, with tongs, without disturbing the fire. Dip the toothed part only in the case-hardening powder for one or two seconds; then carefully withdraw it, so as not to disturb the jacket of powder which has caked around the dipped part. Replace the cutter, teeth down, in the little depression in the fire, which should have remained intact.

This pocket now should hold the cutter blank, with its layer of caked powder, in upright position. As the powder begins to bubble and melt, gently fan the fire to keep the steel dark-yellow hot (even if you do not see it behind that bubbling jacket).

Once the powder has burned off (20 to 30 seconds), immediately quench the hot blank in water (it will sound like a firecracker). Finally, use the regular file-tip test and observe how glassy-hard the teeth have become as a result of this case hardening procedure.

Into the prepared pilot-hole, press a tight-fitting pilot pin made from a $^3/_{16}$-inch spring-steel rod (better for this pin than mild steel). Leave $^1/_2$ inch of the pin protruding. This strong pin will hold the cutter firmly centered during milling.

Similarly, another cutter can be made to countersink holes. A bolt with a round head may be used with six or more teeth, and a pilot pin for exact concentric cutting. The hinge pin riveted during assembly of pliers, for instance, then fills up the cone-shaped space with precise contact surface. This ensures an even bearing as well as holding action for the pliers.

You have now added to your shop a tool accessory essential to the making of precise bearing surfaces for all hinged tools.

Rotary cutters for milling are various and sundry; the design of each one is dictated by the milling job it must perform. You can, for instance, grind a two-bladed cutter with lead pilot out of a ⅜-inch-thick spring-steel blade, as shown. While this is easier to make than the hexagonal cap-screw cutter described above, it is less satisfactory to use in milling seats for hinged tools, since it cuts more slowly and less precisely.

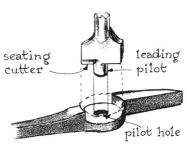

cutting hinge bearing surface for a plier blank

HINGE JOINTS

To make good tongs, pliers, tinsnips, and shears you must be able to make accurate, flat bearing surfaces. It is important to remember that the hinge joints must transfer the force of hand pressure to the blades or jaws of the tool. Thus, the following notes are essential to making the tools described in Chapters 14, 15, 16, and 17, as well as other hinging tools.

An undersized hinge pin tends to bend or break under stress. If the bearing surface between the two halves of the tool is too narrow, the slightest looseness will allow the jaws to flop around. Therefore, a good tool should have oversized (snug-fitting) rather than undersized hinge mechanisms, as well as precise bearing surfaces.

If the bearing surface is 1 inch in diameter and the tool half at that point is ¼ of an inch thick, the hinge pin diameter should not be less than $^5/_{16}$ inch. These dimension relationships are recommended for all such hinged tools, of whatever caliber.

grind flat hinge & blade
surface on side grinder

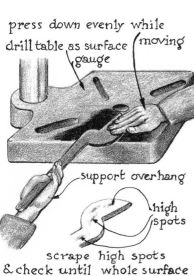

press down evenly while moving
drill table as surface gauge

support overhang

high spots

scrape high spots
& check until whole surface
is accurate. Next, assemble
and drill hinge hole

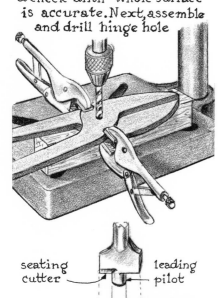

seating cutter — leading pilot

pilot hole

cutting hinge bearing
surface for a plier blank

Making A Strong and Accurate Hinge Joint

The hinging mechanism of a pair of tinsnips is representative of the hinge-joint in many other tools.

Assume both tool halves of your tinsnips are ready as rough blanks, now to be prepared for assembly (see page 70). Make the contact surfaces accurately flat on the side grinder. Test them as follows.

Smear a tiny bit of blackening paste (printer's ink or lampblack mixed with grease) on any surface that you know to be perfectly flat (your drill press table is ideal). Place the ground surface of the blank on it and rub the blank back and forth evenly. Examine it for blackened high spots. Scrape or file these off. (You can make a scraper from an old triangular file that has been ground smooth to make razor-sharp edges.) Scrape and test as many times as necessary, until an even contact indicates that the whole bearing surface is perfectly flat.

An alternative method of making the surface accurate is to place the annealed bearing surface of the blank on the flat face of a hard, unscarred, accurate anvil. Cover it with a piece of flat-surfaced ½-inch-thick steel plate. Strike this hard with a very heavy hammer; one well-centered blow will even out all inaccuracies. A well-annealed steel blank (if no thicker than ¼ of an inch) will respond very well to this treatment.

Refine the surface further either on your side grinder or with a file. The latter method is best done in the vise: make a jig by nailing two ³/₁₆-inch-thick strips of perfectly flat steel 2 inches apart (on either side of the blank) on a small piece of wood. These will guide the file strokes. Clamp the wood level in your vise, and move the file across the blank's bearing surface. As soon as the file begins to graze both strips simultaneously, it has cut away all the excess steel of the hinge-joint area and the filed surface has become accurate and flat as the jig itself.

A third method of making the bearing surface flat is to recess the blank accurately in a flat-planed hardwood jig, dispensing with the steel alignment guides altogether. This is illustrated on page 74.

Other inventive ways to ensure accuracy for flat bearing surfaces may occur to you; however, they will be increasingly less important once your freehand filing skill becomes adequate to do the job.

Assembling the Hinge Joint

When both tinsnip blanks have been accurately refined, clamp them together, as shown, in visegrip pliers. Punch-mark a dead-center location for drilling the hinge-pin hole.

Now drill a preliminary hole with a ¼-inch drill. As a precaution (to cushion the bit when it bores through the steel), clamp an oblong piece of hardwood in the drill vise. This wood "cushion" should be flat-topped and set at a right angle to the drill. Place the hinge joint (still clamped in the pliers) over the wood and drill the premarked hole through both tool halves.

Separate the two blanks and enlarge the ¼-inch hole in one of them with a $^5/_{16}$-inch drill. Thread the other hole with a $^5/_{16}$-inch threading tap to fit the $^5/_{16}$-inch-diameter hinge pin. (In threading holes with taps of ¼ inch diameter or less, I find that approximate sizes are perfectly adequate as long as one proceeds cautiously, little by little, clockwise and counter-clockwise.) If the taps are a little dull, use plenty of lard as a cutting agent and steady, aligned movements during the cutting. If a tap should break off, heat that part in the forge fire, anneal, and drill out the broken tap.

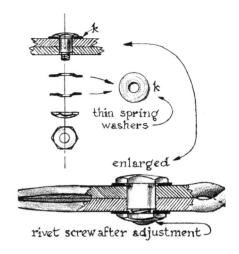

thin spring washers

enlarged

rivet screw after adjustment

You are now ready to assemble the hinge mechanism. Insert the hinge pin and screw into the threaded half. It can now be locked by a nut if you are satisfied the fit is exact and there is no binding friction between the bearing surfaces of the hinge joint.

The locknut and cap-screw system may be improved still further by placing a smooth washer between the cap-screw head and the blank. Lubricated, the hinging action will prove more even, and more lasting in accuracy, with the washer.

Sometimes smooth, unthreaded hinge pins may be riveted on just enough to eliminate any play in the hinge joint. However, in time the rivet head will wear down as it rubs against the blank as the pin turns. Riveted-on countersunk washers will improve this system, as shown. This hinging method is treated in Chapter 15.

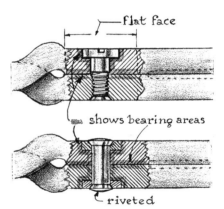

flat face

shows bearing areas

riveted

The above procedures apply to all tools that have similar hinge joints. More elaborate setups are found in carefully machined combination pliers and wire cutters. But all aim at hinging actions that remain smooth, strong, and without play. Play, or slack, causes wobbling and malfunction of the tool.

Depending upon your skill, you can now extend your projects to the making of various hinging tools.

14. Making Tinsnips

Just as with shears, pliers, and tongs, the keystone of a superior pair of tinsnips is its hinge mechanism. From this, all else follows; and, in view of its significance, bear these points in mind as you make your first hinged tool: (1) The hinge joint must have smooth bearing surfaces that stay in contact without play or friction. (2) The hinge pin mechanism must stay in place, not work itself loose under stress or in time. (3) The shank of the hinge pin should be large enough to prevent rapid wear, and fit snugly but not bind. (4) The proper dimensional relationship between hinge-pin diameter and thickness of bearing surface should be observed. (5) From time to time, the whole mechanism should be oiled.

LIGHT-GAUGE TINSNIPS

The stock for such tinsnips can be cut from a salvaged automobile bumper. As a rule, bumper steel is about ⅛ of an inch thick (⅛-inch in small cars; ³/₁₆-inch in heavy trucks). Cut out the section you need with the abrasive cutoff wheel, then heat it evenly in your forge fire. While it is hot, pound it flat on the anvil face and bury it in ashes to anneal.

Cut a cardboard template (pattern), as shown. For symmetrical tinsnips, make a duplicate template. Turn the one over onto the other, and, using a thumbtack as hinge pin, move the cardboard blades in a simulated cutting action.

This allows you to examine the feasibility of your design, and alter it, if necessary. Once you are satisfied with it, scribe the templates on the annealed plate-steel stock. Use either a hacksaw or the abrasive cutoff wheel, to cut out the two blanks.

To make the openings in the handle grips, use a ¼-inch high-speed steel drill at *low* speed, cutting a series of holes around grip openings as shown. Then knock out the waste and file all jagged edges inside and out, so both blanks are completely smooth.

Next, create a jog between the hinge part and the handle by hot-bending the steel; this clears the file strokes during the filing of the hinge bearing surface. This hinge bearing surface and blade must be accurately filed flat. File freehand, if you have developed that skill, or use a jig, as shown, if it gives you more confidence.

Next the file texture is removed by grinding gently on the side grinder or scraping with a triangular scraper. Use the test for flatness (on a blackened surface gauge, as described on page 72).

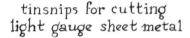

tinsnips for cutting light gauge sheet metal

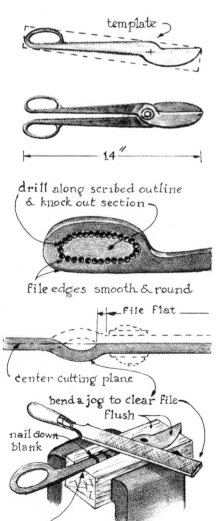

template

⊢————— 14″ —————⊣

drill along scribed outline & knock out section

file edges smooth & round

file flat

center cutting plane

bend a jog to clear file flush

nail down blank

recess wood to hold blank for accurate filing.

74

Now clamp the blanks together with visegrip pliers, in mock assembly, and center them on the drill press table with its woodblock prop. Drill a ¼-inch-diameter hole through both blades and put in a temporary ¼-inch hinge pin that fits snugly. Remove the pliers (see also page 72). Heat the tool handles in the forge fire for final bending. Clamp the hot handles in the vise and force them into alignment between the vise jaws. (The blades are twisted similarly into that same alignment.) Then disassemble the blades and prepare for *hollow grinding*.

Hollow-Grinding the Cutting Blades

Begin the hollow grinding of the blade on your ½ hp grinder, using a large, extrafine-grit wheel. Before you begin grinding, make sure the tool rest almost touches the wheel. (If there is a gap, the blade tends to become wedged into the opening.) Place the blade gently against the wheel so that its spine is on the tool rest and its cutting edge is upright and just clear of the spinning wheel face. This position places the flat of the blade against the grindstone, so that a hollow impression is ground in the inner surface of the blade, all along it, but stopping $1/16$ of an inch short of the cutting edge, and just short of the hinge bearing surface (see illustrations). Similar results can be obtained by filing at a slight slant, as shown. Hollow grinding ensures that only the actual *cutting* edges (instead of the flats) of the blades are in contact once the tool is assembled.

Please note that extreme care should be taken while grinding, so you do not "run over," into either the hinge area or the $1/16$-inch cutting edge. If you overgrind in either direction, you will destroy the accuracy of the hinge bearing surface or the accuracy of the cutting edge — or both. In either case, the blades will not properly "meet," hence cannot cut or shear at that point.

Since the steel has been annealed, you can cold-bend a slight curve in each blade after hollow-grinding or filing. This curve dictates the amount of pressure exerted by the blade's cutting edge, but only experience can tell you just how *much* of a curve is needed. In general, however, the degree of curve is determined by thickness and hardness of the metal to be cut, as well as length and springiness of the tinsnip blade itself.

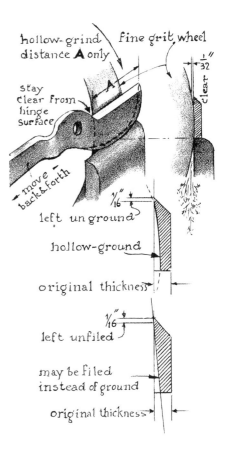

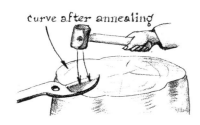

curve after annealing

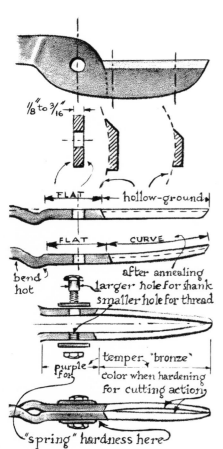

1/8" to 3/16"

FLAT — hollow-ground

FLAT — CURVE

bend hot

after annealing

larger hole for shank
smaller hole for thread

purple for

temper "bronze"
color when hardening
for cutting action

"spring" hardness here

Curving the Blades

While the blade is still annealed, place it on the wood stump, with the inside facing up and the hinge area free, as shown. Using a 1½-pound wooden mallet, pound fairly heavily on the blade, working from the hinge area toward the tip. Sight the gradually forming curve in the blade from time to time, until you believe it to be sufficient.

If the steel is too thin around the hinge point, it may produce too springy a blade. This can be partially corrected by use of a hinge screw and sturdy, large-diameter washers that fit snugly.

Tempering the Blade

Temper the blade and hinge area, heating evenly to a light-cherry-red heat glow, and quench.

It is at this point that we encounter the endless controversy on how best to quench a delicate, thin, and long steel part so that its original shape will be least affected by the uneven shrinkage that causes warping.

Should the curve in the blade warp radically after the quench, all you can do is reheat, reestablish the intended curve, and try slanting the blade at a different angle in the quenching bath. A lopsided slant *may* compensate for an unsymmetrical blade, so that the surfaces that shrink first can achieve the curve originally intended.

Here experience is not always reliable, since you are probably working with unknown types of steel from your scrap pile. One piece may be a typical water-hardening steel, another, an oil-hardening type. The best you can do is experiment, hoping that an undistorted brittle-hard blade will finally emerge from the quench. Only then can you proceed to carefully polish, clean, and temper the blade for specific hardness.

Drawing Temper Colors

Begin by holding the *hinge* part over the heat core, far enough from the flame to ensure slow heating. At the first sign of a faint straw color, move the blade part slowly back and forth through the heat core, until a light straw color indicates that the whole blade is uniformly drawn. Keep heating it very gradually until you see the color changes from light straw to dark straw to bronze. At this point withdraw the blade and let it cool at room temperature for about a minute, *without* quenching.

While the tool is still fairly hot, hold it by the blade and return it to the heat core, so that the handle part bordering the hinge area will heat to a peacock to dark purple. When this color spreads over the hinge area, that portion then has achieved a "spring" hardness, which will prevent the blade from breaking at the hinge, where strain is generally the greatest. The balance of the handle remains annealed, as before. All that is left is to assemble the tool, as detailed in Chapter 13 (see page 70), on making hinge joints.

The hinge pin used with washers and lock nut (see page 73) is especially suited for light-gauge tinsnips. A $^5/_{16}$-inch-diameter cap screw which has a smooth shank acts as the bearing for one blade in a $^5/_{16}$-inch hole; the threaded portion of the cap screw fits the threaded hole in the other blade. The hinge pin should be long enough to allow room for a smooth washer to be inserted between cap-screw head and one blade, and for a flat locknut to be added to the outside of the other blade.

HEAVY-DUTY TINSNIPS

The only difference between light and heavy tinsnips is the gauge of stock used to make them. More rigid blades and hinge joints that will stay in contact while cutting heavier sheet metal require heavier-gauge steel. Such snips can be used to cut small nails and thin wire, as well as heavier sheet metal. As stock, use car leaf springs no less than ¼ of an inch thick. If you do not use the abrasive cutoff wheel, the blank can be cut by a welder with a cutting torch.

The thicker the sheet metal to be cut, the sturdier and longer the handles will have to be, in order to provide enough leverage to cut comfortably by hand.

Curving such thick blades will be difficult unless you heat them first, but take great care not to distort the flatness of the hinge bearing surface.

Draw the cutting edges of heavy tinsnips to a light straw temper color (after brittle quenching), and the rest of the tool to peacock.

The Hinge

The thicker steel involved here may require a countersunk cap-screw type of hinge pin.

This flat, thin, screw-driver slotted head can be sunk flush in one blade, as in the illustration on page 73; but it may instead bear on the outer surface of the blade, without being countersunk, if you feel that the head of the cap-screw will not be in the way.

The second blade has a threaded hinge hole into which the threaded end of the cap screw fits, adjusted so that the blades will bear on one another but not bind. Enough threaded section must protrude to be riveted flush with the countersunk hole on the outer surface of the blade.

One advantage of this adjustable hinge pin is that future slack, through wear, may be taken up by tightening the screw a little, and riveting the protruding thread-end flatter. When properly adjusted, there should be just enough clearance between the bearing surfaces to prevent any hinge wobble or faulty alignment during cutting. And finally, remember that occasional lubrication will extend the life of your hinge mechanism.

Should you find that "naked" handle grips are rough when you are cutting great amounts of heavy metal, try winding them with soft leather thong.

Having successfully completed a pair of heavy-gauge tinsnips, you are thoroughly prepared for making the many other tools that employ a hinging, cutting, or gripping action. Now try your hand at making scissors, nail- and wire cutters, shears, pliers, or tongs.

Leather thong winding

15. Making Wire and Nail Cutters

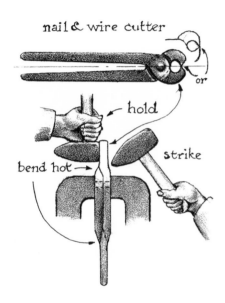

nail & wire cutter

hold

bend hot →

strike

NARROW-JAWED CUTTERS

Use as stock a leaf spring from a heavy-duty truck; such steel is apt to be ⅜ to ½ inch thick. After the leaf spring has been heated, flattened, and annealed in ashes, make a cardboard template (following the symmetrical design shown) and scribe it on the steel stock.

Use a ¼-inch high-speed drill, run at slow speed, to cut out the tool blank (a ⅛-inch drill breaks too easily should it bend). The waste pieces can simply be knocked off if only paper thin sections are left between the holes. For greater accuracy, mark off all hole locations beforehand with center-punch depressions. The drill then does not wander and interfere with the previous hole. If it should, withdraw it, turn the blank over, and punch-mark that side accurately. Then drill from that side, to meet the opposite hole halfway. (Another way of controlling a drill that tends to wander is to plug the adjacent hole with a tight-fitting pin, flush with the blank surface. Then readjust the punch mark and redrill accurately, using lard as a cutting agent: it works better than regular machine oil.)

If the drill holes were not spaced closely enough, the steel in between may have to be cut through part-way with a cold chisel. The waste can then be knocked off without difficulty.

If the drilling method seems too much work, try the abrasive cutoff wheel. With thick steel, however, this too may take more effort than you care to spend, and the welder's cutting torch would then be the answer.

Once the blank has been cut out, grind all edges smooth and drill the temporary hinge holes. These must match the diameter of the lead-pilot of the seating cutter which you will use later on instead of a file to mill a clean face on the hinge bearing surface.

Now assemble the two blanks with a snug-fitting temporary hinge pin, to hold them together while hot-bending their jaws. Clamp the hinge part in the vise, and use two hammers, as shown, to align the yellow-hot jaws. The jaws can be further adjusted to make the cutting edges meet.

Now heat the handles and clamp their hot ends in the vise. The visegrip pliers, holding the hinge assembly firmly clamped together, are used to twist it into alignment with the yellow-hot handles.

Next, knock out the temporary hinge pin so that the hinging surface of both blanks can now be milled with the milling cutter. Adjusted to the slowest drill speed, the milling cutter is used only to clean the surface, barely cutting the steel, to produce an accurate bearing surface.

Once more assemble the two blanks, with the holes aligned, and firmly clamp them in visegrip pliers (as shown with the light-gauge tinsnips, page 74). Place the assembly on the accurate wood prop on the drill press table, and drill the final hinge hole.

The remaining steps in finishing nail- and wire cutters follow the procedure described for making tinsnips: tempering, making a permanent hinge pin, fitting the hinge mechanism in exact adjustment with a locknut (see page 73).

WIDE-JAWED CUTTERS

For wide-jawed nail- and wire cutters use the same stock, but leave the blank end wider. This end of the blank, where the jaws are to be, can be twisted hot, as the illustration shows. Reheat the twisted jaw and hammer it over a forming rod held in the vise to make the proper curve.

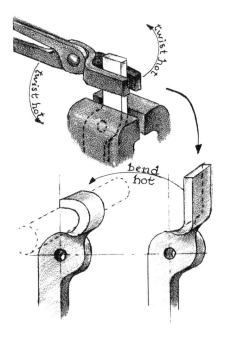

Once both blanks have been identically curved, the remaining steps duplicate those for making the narrow-jawed cutter: assemble with temporary hinge pin; heat, clamp in vise, align hinging part, jaws, and handles with the two-hammer and vise action: file cutting edges on the jaws where they must meet precisely; disassemble and mill clean each hinge bearing surface with the seating cutter.

Reassemble, between visegrip pliers, and drill final hinge hole to receive a rivet-type hinge pin, as shown on page 73.

With washer-size seating cutter, countersink each hinge hole about ⅛ inch to receive washers. Each washer should be countersunk to receive a sturdy rivet head. These heads can be cold-riveted with the hammer peen, then evened out flush with the blade surface with the hammer face. Using a few drops of kerosene as a flushing agent, open and close the hinge forcefully to wear down any unevenness that may cause binding. Flush out any metal pulp with more kerosene.

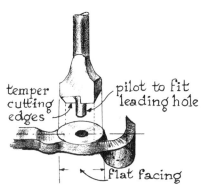

Continue this riveting and "wearing" until the hinge action is snug but easy-moving. All bearing surfaces should be seated without undue slack.

This hand-fitting will prove to be as good — or better — than elaborate machine-fitting, and it will approximate the accuracy of hand-seating engine valves with abrasive compounds. Do not, however, use abrasive compounds in these particular hinge mechanisms, since they would wear down the pin itself, and so ruin the fine fit between pin and hole.

16. Making Large Shears

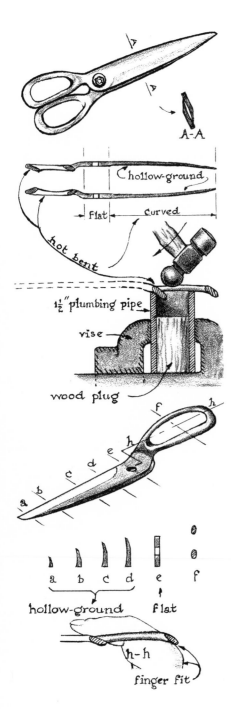

Ordinary household scissors are made in the same way as large shears. Use a portion of a salvaged car bumper about $3/16$-inch-thick as stock, or a section cut from a plow disc. Heat the stock and straighten out its curve on the anvil, then anneal slowly, in ashes.

As these shear blades will be symmetrical, make two cardboard templates and assemble them with a thumbtack to see whether the design needs correction or improvement.

Scribe the outlines for the two blanks on the annealed, flattened stock. (A discarded dental tool or ice pick makes a good scribe.) Cut out the blanks on your abrasive cutoff wheel, or use a hacksaw. True up the blanks on the grinder, or with a file, until all edges are smooth and exact. Cut out the handle grips and smooth them as described on page 74.

Now heat the handle grip to a dark yellow heat glow and place it, as shown, over the tube (a plumbing-pipe forming bar, reinforced with a wood plug) clamped in the vise. Using the ball end of a one-pound hammer, bend the parts of the steel over the tube rim so that hand and fingers will not have to encounter sharp edges when you use the shears.

Hollow-grind and curve the blades as with the tinsnips (page 75). However, since shears have longer blades than tinsnips, they will require even greater observation and corrective manipulation during quenching for hardness to prevent warping. Distortion is probably best avoided by using an oil quench.

Once the blade emerges brittle-hard, and with its intended curve intact, buff it mirror-smooth, before temper colors are drawn. Draw color exactly as with the light-gauge tinsnips, but take extra care to draw the bronze color as evenly as possible over the whole blank.

Now draw the hinge bearing surface locally, to purple, to ensure adequate spring action in that area. For this localized drawing of color, the small, concentrated flame of a propane torch, held about 4 or 5 inches away, is most effective.

The only difference in procedure between the hinge design of these shears and that of light-gauge tinsnips is in the size of the hinge pin and the type of washer used. For the shears, the hinge pin shank acts as a bearing in *both* blanks instead of only the one. Just enough thread should protrude at its far end for a flat locknut to be added, as shown.

Instead of the straight, flat washers of the tinsnips, shears should use "spring-action" washers (see page 73). These exert an inherent spring pressure between the flat hinge surfaces. Once correct pressure is established, the protruding thread is riveted flush with the nut, locking the pin to prevent its working loose. As always, lubricate all hinge bearing surfaces.

Poorly made shearing tools often suffer from short-lived hinging mechanisms, generally because the cap screw is too small in diameter. This requires the threaded part of the screw, riveted into the blank, to be frequently adjusted to take up the slack between blades. Such blades tend to wobble and cut poorly at best, and their thin hinge pin often bends under strain.

So, at the risk of repetition, bear in mind that, *if* the steel is sound and not too thin, *if* the steel is tempered correctly, *if* the blades are curved and hollow-ground to the proper degree, then only the *hinge mechanism* can be at fault, if the tool malfunctions.

17. Making Pliers

There is a wide choice of possible designs for pliers, but as your first project make a simple pair of symmetrical ones.

You will need a speed-reducing transmission device for your drill press (available through some mail-order houses that feature power-tool accessories). Just as the lowest gear in a truck transmission exerts maximum pull, so will this reduction device slow down even the lowest speed in a standard ½ hp drill press. This slow, powerful action is needed when a hinge seating has to be milled in steel as thick as plier blanks. (It is also essential in other shop projects, such as when using large drills, which would quickly dull if run at high speed in heavy going.)

PLIER BLANKS

For pliers to be of high quality, the all-important consideration, of course, is a hinge mechanism that fits snugly, without wobble. The diameter of your seating cutter (one inch, for instance) determines the size of the hinge and, in turn, the size of the pliers.

Choose a piece of spring steel, about ⅜ of an inch thick and 2½ inches wide. Heat an 8-inch length, flatten it on the anvil, and anneal it as soft as possible (cooled slowly, while buried in ashes).

Scribe the two blanks from the cardboard template you designed beforehand, being sure to allow a $1^1/_{16}$- to 1⅛-inch diameter in the hinge seating area.

Cut out the blanks as described earlier, in the sections on tinsnips and shears.

Drill a ¼-inch-diameter hinge hole in the center of each blank to receive the ¼-inch-diameter milling cutter pilot (see page 71). The pilot anchors the seating cutter so that it remains centered while seating the hinge bearing surface.

If you want to relieve your seating cutter of some of the work in cutting, pre-scribe the exact one-inch circle around the pilot hole. Within that circle, drill (with a ¼-inch drill) as many ⅛-inch-deep depressions as you can fit. By thus "pitting" the area, only a small amount of steel remains to be milled away by the seating cutter to reach a $^3/_{16}$-inch depth.

Search in your scrap pile for a 1-inch-diameter rod to match the 1-inch-diameter seating depression of the plier blank. Cut a 3-inch length of that rod and file or grind its end flat, to form a precise right angle with its length.

Seat the rod in the plier hinge depression, and clamp it in the vise. Then, using this jig as a file rest and guide, file off any steel in excess of the 1-inch hinge diameter.

Now assemble both blanks with a temporary ¼-inch bolt, and, with some abrasive valve-grinding compound (available in automobile-parts stores) smeared on the flat bearing surfaces only, grind in the hinge surfaces precisely. When you are satisfied with their seating, disassemble the plier blanks and clean all abrasive remnants away with a little cleaning solvent. Countersink the hinge holes slightly in their outer surface, to later receive riveted hinge-pin heads.

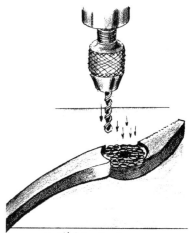

predrill ⅛ inch deep over bearing area for seating-cutter follow up

TEMPERING THE JAWS

Temper the plier jaws as with tinsnips: the jaws, *hard;* the hinge, *springy.* Assemble the plier halves once more and insert the permanent hinge pin; this pin should be a section of annealed, high-carbon ¼-inch-diameter rod, long enough so that its ends can be riveted into heads on the outside of the pliers.

Place the assembly on the anvil face and rivet the end of the pin with the ball end of a ball-peen hammer, striking in the center of the pin to spread it a little; then use the flat of the hammer to "stretch" the outer rim of the pin still further. Alternate hammering with the ball and the flat — now on one end of the pin, now on the other. In due time, this combined hammering and stretching of the pin's head will fill the counter sunk depression in the hinge. Any excess rivet-head steel can be filed off, flush with the plier surface. From time to time open and close the pliers to test the snugness of the hinge fit, and oil generously, to work in all bearing surfaces.

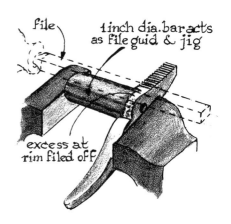

File

1 inch dia. bar acts as file guid & jig

excess at rim filed off

The area of the pin heads, where these touch the steel surfaces of the countersunk holes, also acts as an important bearing surface. But the side strain placed on plier jaws is minimal compared to the pincer strain placed on the hinge mechanism. Thus your major consideration remains: the precise fit of all hinge bearing surfaces, which is what makes one pair of pliers better than another.

ALIGNING JAWS AND HANDLES

Once you find that the hinge assembly functions correctly, but jaw and handle are slightly misaligned, correct this by cold bending. First, make certain that the hinge area is tempered "springy" (purple to blue). Only plier jaws are to be tempered hard (bronze).

Bear in mind that unannealed high-carbon steel that is tempered springy may break during bending. Therefore, if significant bending is required, it is better to anneal the tool first, bend it correctly, then retemper it afterward. Major realignment should only be done by clamping the hinge section in the vise; then use a large pipe as a lever to bend jaw or handle into line, if you are certain that the steel next to the hinge will "give" a little without breaking.

If the tool parts are only slightly off-line, or if you are afraid of breaking the tool during bending, try grinding the excess off on the side grinder when the pliers are permanently assembled.

If you have a saw table, an excellent way to align jaws is to substitute a thin plastic abrasive disc for the circular saw blade. Lay the assembled pliers, fastened with a temporary hinge pin, flat on the saw table. Check to see if the two plier elements are flush with one another. If they are not, it means that the hinge seating depressions were not cut to exactly half the thickness of the plier blanks.

True up the difference by grinding the temporarily assembled pliers on the side grinder, as shown.

When they are accurately aligned, place the pliers open and flat on the saw table. While the thin plastic abrasive disc turns at full speed, the opened plier jaws are now gently closed on the spinning abrasive disc. Any remaining inaccuracy of jaw alignment will in this manner be ground off both jaws simultaneously.

Once the whole tool is polished again, you can restore color and give it a beautiful finish as described in Chapter 18.

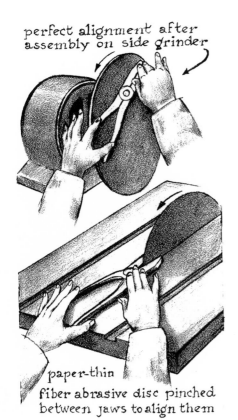

perfect alignment after assembly on side grinder

paper-thin fiber abrasive disc pinched between jaws to align them

18. Applying Color Patina to Steel Surfaces

Oxidation colors that appear on steel surfaces during the tempering process are, in effect, color patinas. Their beauty, no doubt, has already impressed you during the foregoing tempering exercises; it may have occurred to you that such colors can be restored to the finished tool. Mild-steel tools as well as high-carbon ones can be colored this way.

Suppose, for example, that a long-used, well-tempered tool has lost its surface color through wear, and become a bit rusty here and there. Simply rebuff the whole surface to the mirror sheen it had before tempering, making sure you do not overheat it so as to destroy its temper.

Now, holding it over a gas flame, you can actually "color" the whole tool just to please the eye. But here be warned that the *hard* part of the tool must be colored only within the *yellow* range (matching the critical temperature for that hardness), in order not to lose its correct temper. All other areas may be patinated to your taste, again and again, without harm to either tool or cutting edge.

The steel handles of pliers, shears, scissors, and tinsnips may, if you feel like it, have graduated colors: light yellow at the jaw or cutting ends; darker yellow at the hinge (the mild-steel pin will become blue); peacock at the midway point on the handles; purple, farther along the handles to, finally, blue at their very tip.

These patina colors, breathtakingly beautiful as they are, are only mildly functional: the patina is a slight protection against rust.

In olden days, the steel of gun barrels was often colored in this way. But nowadays color-patina chemicals in liquid form have become commercially available and can be applied "cold" by gun fanciers. I do not practice this, since I prefer the natural drawing of colors through heating the steel, with end results that have always proved very satisfying.

It is here that the good craftsman, the "artisan," blends craft with art; when pleasure in aesthetics is a bonus added to the pleasure of making things.

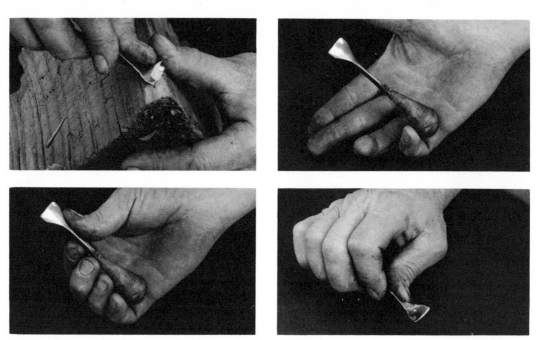

The small woodcarving gouge is manipulated in the same way as the engraver's burins. The flat upright slides along thumb during each stroke of the tool.

The engraving reproduced here was engraved on endgrain wood, using traditional burins. The burin's flat upright allows it to slide along the thumb during the tool's cutting strokes.

Bali Bella Donna, *endgrain wood. Engraving, 7½x12.*

Testing cone design of gouge, cutting an S-curve through splintery, soft, redwood board. The bevel edge is on the outside. The slant of the edge is an original design feature described in Chapter 12.

Mother and Child. Java teakwood, lifesize. The woodcarving gouges described in Chapter 12 were used to carve this sculpture.

Stonecarving tools made as described in Chapter 5 were used to carve this lifesize stone sculpture. PHOTO: Jim Ziegler

Hints on Using Power Tools and Other Admonitions

Use safety goggles at all times, especially since you will be using grinding wheels without wheelguards, in order to have full access to them. If you use prescription glasses, wear goggles over them to avoid their being pitted or broken. For long, sustained grinding, also use a nose filter.

Test the grinding wheel for flaws. When balanced in your hand, the stone should "ring" when tapped with a light hammer. If, instead, the sound is "dull," the stone may be cracked and should be *discarded.* Any wheel being used for the first time should be run for a full minute (while you stand aside) before you accept it as sound.

If grinding wheels are used without wheelguards and mounted directly on a ⅓ to ½ hp 1750 rpm motor, use wheels not more than 8 inches in diameter and ¾ of an inch thick, for safety; on a ⅓ to ½ hp 3600 rpm motor, use for safety reasons wheels 6 inches in diameter or less and preferably not less than ¾ of an inch thick.

Keep the gap between stone and tool rest closed. When the tool rest is bolted to the table beneath the stone, as shown in this book, adjust it by tapping it toward the stone until contact produces a few sparks.

The wheel should rotate so that the upper surface revolves toward the operator. Thus, the steel being ground will be held pressed on the tool rest.

If you use the *sides of the wheel,* do it sparingly, with very light pressure, to prevent grooving. If the side of the wheel has to be redressed too frequently, it becomes thinner and may fly apart.

If the side of a wheel must be used extensively, use the specially designed side grinder described in Chapter 6.

Always move steel back and forth against the stone, during grinding, to avoid cutting grooves into the stone.

Use hard *coarse-grain stones* (1 inch thick or more) for removing large quantities of steel. Use *fine-grain stones* for delicate, more precise steel removal — and for refining texture preparatory to honing and polishing.

Remember that *motor power* should be utilized to its fullest if you plan to remove quantities of steel effectively. Therefore, bear down hard on the stone while moving steel back and forth (short of slowing down the motor), if steel has not yet been tempered or if it is mild steel.

When grinding tempered tools, always take care that the steel does not lose its hardness through *overheating* during grinding. Cool the steel frequently by quenching. (Mild-steel and unfinished tools, of course, may be overheated since hardening and tempering are still to follow.)

Keep a one-gallon can of water next to your grinder at all times, for cooling workpieces.

Remember that should *oxidation colors* accidentally appear on the cutting part of a tool, the color spectrum will indicate the degree of temper loss: *Yellow* (when cooled instantaneously) means the tool still remains sufficiently hard; *bronze* is a little less hard, but still safe; *dark purple* is almost too soft for cutting steel; *light blue* means you have lost your tool hardness at that spot.

If hardness remains unaffected behind the softened cutting edge, grind the tool back to the point of remaining hardness. This means losing some of the lifetime of the tool, but no retempering is needed.

Be careful, this time, to cool the tool frequently in order not to overheat again. The new cutting edge should be ground entirely free of the soft portion.

Should accidental overheating anneal too much of the blade, it is best to retemper the tool to ensure its longevity.

Keep adding useful equipment to your shop (once you learn which articles really help save time and muscle). Instead of buying tools, always consider making them yourself. It may be less difficult than you think, and while you will derive pleasure in their making, you will simultaneously improve your skills and gain confidence for still more challenging projects.

Files will often remove steel as efficiently as grindstones — generally as quickly, and with greater control. Don't neglect learning how to file accurately. Make yourself carry out, at least once, the exercises recommended in dealing with hinged tools like tinsnips, shears, pliers, etc. Try to master the filing technique, for it will benefit all you plan to accomplish in toolmaking.

For the serious student, who wants to perfect his filing, write to file manufacturers for their instructive booklets.

When I was a student in Holland, we spent all the shop hours during our whole first year learning only *flat-filing,* so as to achieve machine-like precision. Only after we had acquired that hand skill were we permitted to learn blacksmithing, lathe-turning, drilling, milling, and so forth.

Never walk away from a live fire (forge, torch, or brazier) without a very real awareness of the possible danger. The same holds true for a sharp tool left clamped in a vise.

The sound toolmaker is always in absolute control. Distractions lead to accidents — to yourself, to others, and to your tools. Proper care and concentration will go a long way toward toolmaking that is neither hesitant nor mistake-ridden.

Glossary

ADAPTER. A driven instrument made to fit one type (size) of tool at one end and another type (size) at the other end.

AGITATOR. See *Paint Mixer*.

ALIGNMENT. In line with another element; not askew in relation to it.

ALLOY. A compound or fusion of two or more metals.

ANGLE IRON. Steel bars which have a cross-section of an angle (usually 90°). The iron, in this term, is a holdover from the days before iron was made into steel. Now all angle iron is actually steel, either mild or high-carbon steel.

ANNEAL. To soften steel through slow cooling after enough heat has made the steel lose its brittleness.

ARBOR. A wheel, axle, or shaft rotating in one or more bearings held by a frame that is bolted down.

BASTARD FILE. A file with teeth coarser than a smooth file and less coarse than a coarse file.

BEVEL. In cutting tools, the facet that has been ground at the cutting edge (inside and outside *bevels*).

BLANK. The rough shape of a tool before filing, grinding, etc. has prepared the tool for tempering and assembly with the handle.

BOSS. A locally raised part of steel.

BRITTLE QUENCH. See *Quench*.

BUFFER. A cotton wheel used to polish surfaces.

BUNSEN BURNER. A gas burner with a single blue flame used in laboratories to heat liquids and objects.

BURIN. The cutting tool of an engraver.

BURR. A small rotary file, often used to take off a *burr* left on the edge of steel by previous cutting. A *burr* may also be the "feather-edge" left on a tool's cutting edge in the final step of sharpening the tool.

BUSH HAMMER. A tool with a hammer face having 9 or more raised points which, on impact, crush or pulverize the surface of stone. From the French *boucher:* to crush, to eat, to bite. The bush *tool* also has 9 or more raised points which, when hammered upon, crush or pulverize the surface of stone.

BUTTERFLY-CENTER. A lathe-center insert placed in headstock that has four sharp wings and a center pin which press into the wood that is to be turned on a wood lathe.

CAP SCREW (OR TAP-BOLT). A bolt (without its nut) screwed into a threaded hole of one part, to hold another part clamped onto the first.

CARBIDE-TIP. An extremely hard tip soldered on to the end of a regular high-carbon steel bar used to turn wood or steel on a lathe.

CASE HARDENING. The process of applying a skin-deep hardness to the outer surface of mild steel in a forge fire.

CENTER-PUNCH. Tool used to make a "center" mark for locations to be drilled, or to mark off pattern outlines on steel.

CHASING TOOLS. Tools used to make marks (raised or depressed) in metal surfaces to create texture.

CHISEL, CARPENTER'S WOOD. A flat chisel for cutting wood.

CHISEL, COLD. A chisel that may be used on *cold* annealed steel to cut it.

CHISEL, HOT. A chisel used to cut *yellow hot* steel. The steel is cut with the hot chisel on the soft anvil table or a mild-steel plate placed over the hard anvil face. The chisel is either a hand-held long cold chisel or a sturdy chisel head fastened to a long wooden stem.

CHUCK. A clamp screwed on a rotating shaft to fasten drills, small grinders, etc.

CLAW. A multiple-toothed stonecarving tool used to refine the rough texture left by the one-point tool.

COEFFICIENT OF CONDUCTIVITY. A number that indicates the degree of speed at which heat is conducted from one spot to the next in a type of steel.

COIL SPRINGS. Springs made of long, high-carbon steel rods that are wound hot around a bar and afterward tempered the hardness for which such springs are designed.

COLLAR. A steel ring, often mounted on a shaft with a set screw.

CONDUIT PIPE. Galvanized steel pipe through which electricians install electric wires.

COUNTERSINK. A cone-shaped, large *drill bit* used to bevel the edge of a sharp-edged cylindrical hole left by a smaller drill; a shallow cylindrical depression around a hole, larger than the hole in diameter.

CUTOFF WHEEL. A thin abrasive wheel that cuts steel too hard to cut with a hacksaw.

COKE. The substance fresh coal becomes after heat has driven out all elements that give off smoke and yellow flame. Coke resembles charcoal in that it gives off a blue flame and lights easily.

DOWEL (STEEL). A locking-pin that holds parts and keeps them from shifting their positions.

DRAWING TEMPER COLOR. Reheating brittle-quenched steel that has been polished to see the oxidation color spectrum (temper colors) clearly. Once this color spectrum appears and the wanted color, which corresponds to its *hardness*, has been "drawn," the tool is quenched.

DRAWING-OUT STEEL. *Stretching* steel, making it longer or wider or both. The opposite is to upset steel, making it thicker and/or shorter.

DRESSER. A tool that cuts or wears down the surface of grindstones.

DRESSING. Making an inaccurate grinding wheel accurate with a dresser by wearing the wheel surface down to exact shape.

DRILL BIT. Could be called a *drill*, but generally this term refers to a local *bit* at end of a plain drill rod. Such bits may be of varied designs to meet various drilling problems.

DRILL PRESS. A machine for drilling holes in metal or other material.

EMBOSS. To raise steel locally with bosses. The *boss* is a form of die which, pressed or hammered into the steel plate from one side, raises the steel surface on the other side of the sheet.

EYEBOLT. A bolt which has a hole in a round, flattened end instead of the hexagon, or round, or square-bolt head.

FACE. Generally refers to a flat surface on the sides or top of a tool or machine part: an anvil face, side-face, the face of a disc, "to face" a surface, when grinding, milling, and cutting steel surfaces.

FERRULE. A metal ring, cap, or tube-section placed on the end of a handle to keep it from splitting.

FIREBRICK. A brick which withstands high temperatures as in brick-lined kilns and fireplaces.

FIRECLAY. A clay which will not crack when fired.

FORGE. A furnace in which steel is heated.

FREEZING. The bonding together of two clamped-together steel parts that have corroded or have been forcefully locked together. To break this bond is a frequent chore when taking rusted machinery apart.

GAUGE. A specific size in reference to steel sheet or bar thickness, nail size, etc.

HACKSAW. A hand saw with narrow blade set in metal frame, used to cut metal.

HEADSTOCK. The rotating driver end of a lathe.

HEATING. The period of heating the steel.

HEAT. The period that the hot steel, removed from the fire, maintains its forging heat.

HEAT-TREATING. The process of *tempering* steel for a specific hardness; can also refer to treating steel to bring about a specific softness.

HIGH-CARBON STEEL. A temperable steel, primarily used to harden such steels for specific hardness in the process called "tempering." In industry, steel of over 0.2% carbon.

HOLLOW-GRIND. To grind the bevel of a cutting tool concave.

HONING. Grinding a steel surface with a *honing stone*. This stone leaves an almost-polished surface.

HP (HORSEPOWER). A unit of power, used in stating the power required to drive machinery.

JIG. A device which acts as a guide to accurately machine-file, fold, bend, or form a workpiece. This is used if lack of skill handicaps the worker in making the workpiece. Such jigs guide him and also save time in mass production of tools.

LATHE. A machine for shaping articles which causes them to revolve while acted upon by a cutting tool.

LEAF SPRING. A spring with an oblong cross-section and a sufficient length to act as a spring. Automobiles as a rule use such springs singly or in graduated layers to suspend the car body over the axles.

LOW-CARBON STEEL. A steel that is not temperable, which contains less than 0.2% carbon.

MALLEABLE. Capable of being shaped or worked by hammering, etc.

MALLET. A wooden hammer-head on a short handle used to hammer on wood-carving gouges. Sometimes the mallet head is made of rawhide or plastic or hard rubber.

MILD STEEL. A low-carbon steel. It is not temperable.

MILLING CUTTER. See *Seating Cutter*.

NAIL SET. A tool resembling a center-punch but with a hardened, cup-shaped end instead of a ground point. This cup-shaped end, placed on the nail head center, keeps the tool from slipping sideways while "setting" the nail.

ONE-POINT TOOL. The basic stonecarving tool that "chips" stone in the first roughing-out action of stonecarving.

OXIDATION COLOR SPECTRUM. The color spectrum that results from the oxidation of cold steel as it gradually gets hot. The polished metal sheen shows the colors as clearly as the color spectrum in rainbows.

PAINT MIXER (AGITATOR). A rod with a crooked end which, rotated in the paint, mixes it.

PATINA. The colored oxidation on metal surfaces. It results during the process of tempering the metal. (On bronze and many other metals, a patina comes about after long exposure to oxygen of the air and chemicals.)

PEARL GRAY. A typical file color. When high-carbon steel emerges from a quench, pearl gray indicates "file hardness."

PEEN END. A hammer with a wedge-shaped, round-edged end or a half-sphere ball end used to stretch steel by indentation. A *cross peen* hammer has the rounded edge of the peen at 90° to the hammer stem.

PUSH-ROD. The rod in an engine which "pushes" a valve to open the cylinder for the intake or expulsion of its gases.

QUENCH. To cool hot steel in a liquid. *Brittle quenching* is the act of cooling high-carbon steel at its critical heat at its fastest so that it will emerge brittle-hard.

QUENCHING BATH. The liquid into which the hot steel is dipped or immersed to cool it.

RASP. A coarse file used mostly to grate or tear softer materials such as wood, horn, plaster of Paris, and soft stones that are not abrasive.

ROUT. To cut or scoop out material with a router tool.

SADDLE. A rounded piece of steel on which to form another piece in its shape.

SCRIBE. A sharp-pointed steel marking pin used to scratch a line on to a work-piece.

SEATING CUTTER. Tool used to cut a *seat* in a part onto which another part fits exactly. The cutting also may be called *milling,* and the cutter then would be a *milling cutter.*

SET SCREW. A screw that clamps or *sets* one part onto another part.

SHANK. The part of a tool between tang and blade.

SHOULDER. In craft usage, an abrupt wider or thicker dimension in rod or shaft against which another part rests.

SPECTRUM. A division of colors occurring on the shiny part of steel when it is heated for tempering; similar to the rainbow colors seen through a prism.

SPRING STEEL. A high-carbon steel tempered so that it will act as a spring.

STEEL PLATE. Refers to flat sheets of steel thicker than $3/16$ of an inch. It is optional at what thickness or thinness metal may be called sheet metal. Example: boilers are made of plate steel; stovepipes are made of sheet metal.

STEEL STOCK. The supply of steel from which an item is selected to forge, or machine, or grind the workpiece to be made.

STROPPING. The final step in sharpening a cutting edge on a leather strop.

TAILSTOCK. The center pin in the stationary end of the lathe that holds the rotating metal, wood or other material between the two lathe centers.

TANG. The part of the tool blank that is locked into the tool handle.

TEMPERABLE STEEL. A steel of a higher than 0.2% carbon quality which can be *tempered.*

TEMPERING. In forging metal, the process to arrive at a specific hardness of high-carbon steel.

TEMPLATE. A pattern, often made from cardboard or sheet metal, to serve as a model, the outline of which is scribed on the steel to be cut.

TOOL REST (OR TOOL POST). As a rule, those parts on machines onto which a tool is held down firmly to be ground down. Also may refer to the clamp on a machine to hold a cutting tool.

TRIPOLI. An abrasive-impregnated wax compound that, when rubbed into a rotating cotton buffing wheel, acts as the finest steel polisher.

UPSETTING. The process of making a piece of steel shorter and thicker.

VEINING TOOL. A V-shaped gouge that cuts V grooves referred to as "veins."

VISE. A two-jawed screw clamp bolted to the workbench to hold things steady while being worked.

VISEGRIP PLIERS. Self-locking pliers.